**London Borough
of Hounslow**

Hounslow Library Servic

KT-428-390

This item should be returned or renewed by the latest date shown. If it is not required by another reader, you may renew it in person or by telephone (twice only). Please quote your library card number. A charge will be made for items returned or renewed after the date due.

⊙ Walking Eye App

YOUR FREE EBOOK AVAILABLE THROUGH THE WALKING EYE APP

Your guide now includes a free eBook to your chosen destination,
for the same great price as before. Simply download the Walking Eye
App from the App Store or Google Play to access your free eBook.

HOW THE WALKING EYE APP WORKS

Through the Walking Eye App, you can purchase a range of eBooks and destination
content. However, when you buy this book, you can download the corresponding
eBook for free. Just see below in the grey panel where to find your free content and
then scan the QR code at the bottom of this page.

Destinations: Download essential destination content featuring recommended sights and attractions, restaurants, hotels and an A–Z of practical information, all available for purchase.

Ships: Interested in ship reviews? Find independent reviews of river and ocean ships in this section, all available for purchase.

eBooks: You can download your free accompanying digital version of this guide here. You will also find a whole range of other eBooks, all available for purchase.

Free access to travel-related blog articles about different destinations, updated on a daily basis.

HOW THE EBOOKS WORK

The eBooks are provided in EPUB file format. Please note that you will need an eBook reader installed on your device to open the file. Many devices come with this as standard, but you may still need to install one manually from Google Play.

The eBook content is identical to the content in the printed guide.

HOW TO DOWNLOAD THE WALKING EYE APP

1. Download the Walking Eye App from the App Store or Google Play.
2. Open the app and select the scanning function from the main menu.
3. Scan the QR code on this page – you will then be asked a security question to verify ownership of the book.
4. Once this has been verified, you will see your eBook in the purchased ebook section, where you will be able to download it.

Other destination apps and eBooks are available for purchase separately or are free with the purchase of the Insight Guide book.

CONTENTS

FOODIES

Reykjavík (route 1) is undergoing a resurgence as a foodie destination with its New Nordic restaurants. Outside the capital, go for lobster in Höfn (route 7), or try an old horror, putrefied shark, at Bjarnarhöfn (route 14).

RECOMMENDED ROUTES FOR...

ISLAND FUN

Visit friendly Heimaey (route 6), under the shadow of a menacing red volcano; Hrísey (route 11) with its tame ptarmigans; or spend a night in the old settlement on Flatey in Breiðafjörður (route 13).

MUSIC LOVERS

Harpa concert hall in Reykjavík (route 3) is a work of art. Summer recitals are held at Seyðisfjörður's Blue Church (route 8); or learn about Icelandic folk music in Siglufjörður (route 11).

NATURAL WONDERS

Rumbling volcanoes and multicoloured mudpots abound round Mývatn (route 10). Hike on a glacier at Skaftafell (route 7), or enjoy epic waterfalls Gullfoss (route 5), Dynjandi (route 13) or Dettifoss (route 9).

PAMPERING

Iceland's many geothermal pools and spas are a bather's delight. Most famous are the Blue Lagoon (route 4) and Mývatn Nature Baths (route 10). Newest is the Beer Spa at Árskógssandur (route 11).

VIKINGS AND SAGAS

Get a saga overview at the Settlement Centre in Borgarnes (route 14), sail to Drangey island (route 12) where gloomy antihero Grettir was exiled, or see Viking artefacts at the National Museum (route 1).

WALKERS

Vatnajökull National Park has beautiful walks and multiday hikes at Skaftafell (route 7) and Jökulsárgljúfur (route 9). Seasoned hikers should head for deserted Hornstrandir (route 13) or the bleak Interior (routes 15 and 16).

WILDLIFE

Húsavík (route 9) is the whale-watching capital of Europe. Bird-watchers are spoilt: see ducks at Mývatn (route 10), skuas at Skeiðarársandur (route 7) or mixed bird cliffs at Látrabjarg (route 13).

INTRODUCTION

An introduction to Iceland's geography, customs and culture, plus illuminating background information on cuisine, history and what to do when you're there.

EXPLORE ICELAND

Iceland is a place of dramatic contrasts: bleak and blasted, yet intensely beautiful; full of grinding ice and fiery eruptions; with a tiny capital city that generates a huge amount of quirky, energetic culture.

Settled by the Vikings, drawn by the allure of a fresh and empty land, Icelanders have always survived on their foresight, imagination and wits. Although Iceland has a long, rich cultural history, stretching back to the Saga Age, it is the land itself, sculpted by the forces of nature into a unique, ever-changing landscape, that tells the country's most compelling story.

GEOGRAPHY AND LAYOUT

Iceland covers 103,000 sq km (40,000 sq miles) of land, but is sparsely populated, with just three people per square kilometre. Sixty-four percent of Icelanders live in the capital area, and five percent in the second northern 'city', Akureyri. The rest of Iceland is empty, save for scattered farms and small fishing villages dotted around the coast. Sixty-two percent of the country is classified as a wasteland: the whole interior is a hostile uninhabited high desert. Europe's largest glacier, Vatnajökull, squats over 8,400 sq km (3,200 sq miles) of the southeast, its subglacial volcanoes wreaking havoc on the surrounding regions when they erupt.

Iceland straddles the North Atlantic Ridge, where two of the tectonic plates making up the Earth's surface are slowly tearing apart. The country is literally being torn in two, widening at a rate of roughly 2cm (0.8ins) annually. Earthquakes and volcanic activity are commonplace along the huge diagonal double-pronged fault line, running from Reykjanes and the Vestmannaeyjar in the southwest to Krafla in the northeast.

In geological terms, Iceland is a mere baby, composed of some of the youngest rocks on earth and still being formed. Over the centuries, eruptions have spewed vast fields of lava across the island's surface and projected choking clouds of ash high into the air, blocking out the sunlight and blighting crops. Every day there are thousands of minor earthquakes and shocks, most of which are only detectable by seismologists.

The presence of so much natural energy just below ground makes it possible not just to see the awesome power of nature in Iceland, but also to feel, hear and smell it.

Nordic houses line Lake Tjörnin, Reykjavík

GETTING AROUND

The Ring Road (or Route 1) circles the edge of the island (although it bypasses the fjords). It was only completed in 1974: before then, shifting sands and glacial floods proved too challenging for the road builders. You can get round the Ring Road by public bus, although services are limited, especially in winter. From Reykjavík, multiple coach tours visit the west and southwest. However, to circle the entire country, a car is the easiest option.

The routes in this guide begin in the capital city. Two walking tours and a fabulous bike ride allow you to familiarise yourself with Iceland's history and culture, and indulge in Reykjavík's quirky cafés, bohemian bars and exciting restaurants. The routes then cover the country in an anticlockwise direction, starting with volatile Reykjanes peninsula, home of the Blue Lagoon. The Southwest route incorporates the Golden Circle, a famous sightseeing tour that takes in three Icelandic treasures – Þingvellir, Geyser and the waterfall Gullfoss.

The routes then follow the Ring Road along the south coast, into a stunningly beautiful glacial wasteland, before taking time to explore the East Fjords and make several day trips around Egilsstaðir. Following that and launching north, we take in Húsavík to watch whales and Mývatn for birdwatching and bubbling volcanic areas, before enjoying

the gentle charms of the 'city' Akureyri. Heading west, through historical fishing villages and past large seal colonies, the routes leave the Ring Road to take in the ups and downs of the remote, raw West Fjords, before exploring mystical Snæfellsnes peninsula and the saga-filled West. The final two routes traverse Iceland's barren interior.

HISTORY

Norwegian Viking Ingólfur Arnarson was the first official settler in Iceland in 874, basing himself in Reykjavík and planting his hay at Austurvöllur; a Viking farmstead and artefacts can be seen at two excellent museums in the city. Other Vikings followed, and a democratic nation was established in 930 with the formation of the Alþingi parliament.

But by the 10th century, the country had become so crowded that Erik the Red abandoned it for Greenland; by the 12th century the trees were all chopped down, forcing Iceland to rely on other countries for fuel, ships and housing; and by 13th century, family feuding tipped the country into civil war. Into the breach stepped the Norwegian king, who generously offered to quell the violence by taking over power.

Control of the country passed to Denmark in 1397, after which things became much worse. Trade embargoes meant Iceland was reliant on Danish ships for supplies – and the ships often failed to arrive. Even the land itself

Sunrise over iceberg-filled Jökulsárlón lagoon

seemed to turn against the Icelanders, with violent volcanic activity – particularly the devastating 1783 Laki eruption – poisoning crops and cattle. You can see the scale of the Laki event all around Kirkjubæjarklaustur, on the south coast.

Life in Iceland was brutally hard. Only with the 19th-century independence movement did a new hope begin to rise, with Iceland finally becoming a republic on 17 June 1944. The country's sudden lurch in status, from a poor, backward rural nation to a modern prosperous one, came with World War II and occupation by American troops, which prompted frenzied building and economic growth. The expanding fishing industry also brought wealth – and bitter strife with Britain, as Iceland sought to defend its precious cod. Today fishing is still important, although tourism is beginning to overtake it, boosted by Iceland's association with international phenomenon *Game of Thrones*.

CLIMATE

Influenced by the warm Gulf Stream and prevailing southwesterly winds, Iceland's temperate oceanic climate is surprisingly mild considering its position on the edge of the Arctic Circle. However, summers are generally cool, and the country is often wet and windy, with weather changing dramatically from day to day, or even hour to hour. Bring clothes for all eventualities.

Around the 21 June solstice, the sun dips below the horizon at midnight and returns at 3am; during those three hours, the land is bathed in a strangely energising twilight. June to August are high holiday season, when visitor numbers and prices shoot up. In contrast, winter is dark: around December 21, the sun rises after 11am and calls it a day at 3.30pm. One consolation is that from September to mid-April it is dark enough to see the northern lights (see page 83).

For the latest weather in Iceland, see www.vedur.is/english.

POPULATION

The population of Iceland is just 338,000 inhabitants, two-thirds of whom live in the capital Reykjavík and its sprawling suburbs. Reykjavík's growth has been fast, from 5,000 inhabitants in 1901, to almost 217,000 in 2016, altering Icelandic society completely. Retirement-age citizens were born and brought up in the countryside; their grandchildren have been raised entirely in the 'concrete lava fields' of the city.

A long history of isolation means that Icelanders are a homogeneous bunch, three parts Viking to one part Celt. They are hardworking and resilient, having survived all sorts of calamities – both natural and induced – throughout the centuries. Today, Iceland ranks at the top end of the OECD Better Life Index, with Icelanders enjoying low unemployment, above-average wealth, health and edu-

Húsavík is one of the best places in Europe for whale watching

cation, and very little pollution. The average life expectancy is a glowing 83 years.

Along with toughness, Icelanders have frequently required inventiveness and imagination to survive, and have developed a strong sense of community along the way. Icelanders stuck together through necessity and overcame impossible odds,

forging for themselves an extremely strong national identity, and a cultural heritage of which they are very proud.

LOCAL CUSTOMS

Although Reykjavík is a city, it retains a small-town feel. Everyone knows

---

DON'T LEAVE ICELAND WITHOUT...

Having a soak in a geothermal pool. There's nothing quite like lazing in a hot tub as snow falls around your ears. The Blue Lagoon is Iceland's most famous geothermal pool; although try Mývatn Nature Baths for a quieter alternative. See page 78.

Glimpsing the northern lights. Visitors often come to Iceland in the darkest winter months simply to try to observe the uncanny lightshow of the aurora borealis. See page 83.

Marvelling at whales. Húsavík, Iceland's 'whale-watching capital', sits on Skjálfandi Bay, rich with plankton and fish. Sail close in old oaken boats, and watch humpbacks breaching, spyhopping and tail-slapping. See page 74.

Learning more about the sagas. Iceland's biggest contribution to world culture, the laconic medieval sagas are filled with fascinating characters and cover a vast sweep of themes. See page 33.

Making a quirky shopping trip. Treat yourself to music, nibbles or a traditional hand-knitted jumper (*lopapeysa*), or indulge in dark fairytale design with fishskin handbags, sulphur bowls and music boxes woven

from feathers. See page 18.

Strolling along a black-sand beach. Violent waves crash along the south coast. As you try to stay upright in the wind, marvel at the fact that no land stands between you and the Antarctic. See page 55.

Walking on a glacier. Rather than being a flat and featureless walk, a strange world of water cauldrons, ridges and crevasses opens up, scattered with ancient volcanic ash and mossy glacial mice. See page 64.

Eating lamb or fish. You can get fresh, high-quality and quite delicious fish, seafood and lamb all over Iceland, although Reykjavík's reborn restaurant scene is perhaps the best place to relish it. See page 118.

Experiencing active volcanoes. Steaming, sulphurous, lava-spewing landscape is all around you. Visit the island of Heimaey, which had a close call in the 1970s, or why not hike up to the Móði and Magni craters, formed in the 2010 Eyjafjallajökull eruption which paralysed Europe's air traffic for six days, and named after the sons of Thor. See page 55.

On the road to nowhere

everyone, and traffic on the main shopping street Laugavegur often comes to a standstill when a driver stops to chat to a friend they've spotted. In such a small place, social cohesion is important: Iceland's swimming pools and hot pots are social centres where people gather to discuss politics, business, gossip and the weather; and every tiny village has its own festivals and celebrations.

Outside the capital, some towns, notably Akureyri in the north, shame some of Reykjavík's energy, but most are happy not even to try. The smaller towns are quiet, compact and neat, often no more than a cluster of colourful houses around a church or shop. The pace of life is slow, and the sense of community strong. Iceland is, on the whole, an informal, egalitarian and familiar society. Everyone from the President down is addressed by their first name.

Iceland is a hardworking Lutheran Protestant country, with something of an ambivalent attitude to alcohol: drinking mid-week is met with faint disapproval; and yet at the weekend, any amount of beer and spirits go. Dining out is not a late-night affair – restaurant kitchens commonly close at 9pm – but weekend brunch with friends is extremely popular.

A high value is placed on culture and education. Today, 10 percent of Icelanders are published authors, and Reykjavík has bookshops, films, concerts and museums galore, the latter free to everyone under 18.

POLITICS AND ECONOMICS

Iceland's national parliament, the Alþingi, is one of the oldest parliaments in the world, founded in 930 not long after the Viking settlement. Today it has 63 MPs, 39 men and 24 women, elected by proportional representation. Elections are held every four years, with a high voter turnout of 81.2 percent at the most recent (2017) election.

Since the last quarter of the 20th century the country has been increasingly outward looking, attracting foreign business and visitors. However, in recent times, Iceland's political and economic fortunes have taken rollercoaster-like ups and downs. The collapse of the banking system during the 2008 worldwide financial crisis revealed that Iceland's prosperity was built on a dangerously vulnerable economic model. In 2009, Jóhanna Sigurðardóttir, the world's first openly gay head of government, was elected to pick up the pieces. Since then, Iceland has gradually been clawing its way back to prosperity, with GDP growth at 1.2 percent in 2012, 4.1 percent in 2015 and 7.2 percent in 2016.

Contemporary Icelandic politics has been rocked by scandal, with two successive governments collapsing. In April 2016, the release of the Panama Papers revealed that Iceland's Prime

Gljúfrafoss waterfall

Isolated Breiðavík beach, West Fjords

Minister Sigmundur Gunnlaugsson, of the centre-right Progressive Party, had failed to declare ownership of an offshore company. He was forced to resign. In September 2017, his successor, Bjarni Benediktsson, of the conservative Independence Party, was also forced out of office after only eight months. This time, a cover-up came to light involving a letter written by the Prime Minister's father in support of a convicted paedophile.

A record eight parties won seats in the Alþingi after the October 2017 election, with none coming close to obtaining a majority. Four-party coalition talks led by the Left-Greens culminated in a broad three-party coalition between the Left-Greens, the Independence Party and the Progressive Party. Left-Green leader Katrin Jakobsdottir was named Prime Minister.

In economic terms, Iceland remains dependent on the fishing industry, but over recent years, its government has been keen to diversify. Some schemes have been highly controversial, such as the hydroelectrically powered aluminium smelting plant in the Eastfjords and the hunt for oil around Jan Mayen Island. Tourism has seen a massive boom in recent years, with tourist numbers almost quadrupling from 2010 (459,000) to 2017 (1.8 million).

TOP TIPS FOR VISITING ICELAND...

Book accommodation ahead. Iceland is a small country that receives almost two million visitors a year. Accommodation is in short supply in summer, so be sure to book ahead. Note that you can often find good discounts with early or online bookings.

Pre-purchase tickets for the Blue Lagoon. The Blue Lagoon has recently revised its ticketing system, meaning you can no longer just turn up to the geothermal spa. Buy tickets ahead of time via the Blue Lagoon website (www.bluelagoon.com).

Bring a swimsuit. A vital piece of clothing – with every new day, a new swimming pool or hot spring beckons.

Layer up. The weather in Iceland changes rapidly. Bring lots of layers, including a good waterproof and windproof coat, even in the height of summer. Don't bother with umbrellas – the wind will instantly turn them inside out.

Light sleepers, beware. Icelanders build thin walls, and the pesky midnight sun shines right through the generally flimsy curtains. Bring ear plugs and an eye mask if the light bothers you.

Drive carefully. If you're hiring a vehicle, be aware that you'll need a four-wheel drive to venture off the main Ring Road (Route 1). Unpaved sections of road can become pot-holed and rutted; drive on gravel with great caution and navigate fording rivers with utmost care. Drink driving is a serious offence, with a zero-tolerance policy in operation – you cannot consume any alcohol and then drive a vehicle.

Freshly baked bread for sale

FOOD AND DRINK

Iceland offers fantastic food, from dare-you-to-eat-it traditional dishes to world-class Nordic cuisine, with fish and lamb ruling the feast. Whether you want gourmet surroundings, kid-friendly dining, a cool bistro or cosy café, Reykjavík has the lot.

Dining out in Iceland has undergone tremendous changes in the past 20 years. The restaurant scene has been hit by a great wave of energy, enthusiasm and experimentation, with new-found gourmet knowledge being applied to traditional ingredients. Reykjavík restaurants are consequently a real treat. Eating out is not cheap, but you are paying for excellent meals made using high-quality ingredients.

Ethical eating

Icelanders rarely eat whale meat *(hval)*: in fact, the commercial whaling industry is largely sustained by tourists. The International Fund for Animal Welfare (IFAW) and Icelandic whale-watching operators run the 'Meet Us, Don't Eat Us' campaign to draw visitors' attention to the problem – see http://icewhale.is.

For centuries, Icelanders have happily munched cute little puffins, caught with giant nets on the cliff tops. In recent years, however, climate change has severely affected breeding colonies, raising ethical questions about whether puffins should still be on the menu.

LOCAL CUISINE

Fresh from the nearest fishing boat or glacial river, Icelandic fish is absolutely delicious. Sheep flocks graze wild in the highlands, eating herbs as well as grass, giving Icelandic lamb an exceptional gamey flavour. Wild berries, used in sauces and puddings, thrive in the cold climate, and are often mixed into *skyr*, a creamy yoghurt.

Look out for ice-cream in the southern pasturelands; langoustines from Höfn; reindeer and pink-footed geese from the eastern highlands; shrimp on the north coast; seabirds' eggs in spring; wild mushrooms in early autumn; and ptarmigan at Christmas.

Most menus offer at least one vegetarian option, but vegan choices may be limited.

WHERE TO EAT

High-end and mid-range restaurants
Most of Reykjavík's top-class restaurants are in the city centre. The New Nordic cuisine movement, with its focus on local, seasonal, sustainable produce, is a major influence. Fish and lamb feature heavily, with more unusual sea urchins, seaweed,

Fine dining in Reykjavík

Fermented shark is a delicacy

birch leaves, angelica and Icelandic moss arranged like works of art on your plate.

If a seven-course gourmet menu is too much, a range of warm, welcoming places serve top-notch food. Seafood restaurants are generally excellent – try Kaffivagninn, Höfnin and Matur og Drykkur. Family-friendly restaurants offer burgers, pizza and pasta. Bistros do a great job of reinventing old dishes: try *kjötsúpa* (meat soup), *plokkfiskur* (fish stew), reindeer burger or even Arctic char smoked over sheep dung!

Cafés, café-bars and bakeries

Iceland's cafés and bars are fabulously cosy and cheerfully multipurpose – many will serve you coffee and cake for elevenses, soup at lunchtime, tapas for tea, then turn into a banging nightspot.

Bakeries are a positive by-product of Danish rule (1380–1918) – don't leave without gorging on *vínarbrauð*, Iceland's version of Danish pastries.

Fast food

Iceland has rejected McDonalds, sticking to its own versions of fast food. The Icelandic hot dog, loaded with toppings, reigns supreme – Bæjarins Beztu, near Kolaportið flea market, is the capital's go-to late-night hot-dog stand.

DRINKS

Coffee is the national drink of Iceland, consumed at all hours of the day and night.

Wine is imported and eye-wateringly expensive. Between 1915 and 1989, beer was illegal in Iceland, but now makes up 62% of the alcohol drunk by Icelanders. In Reykjavík, a growing craft-beer culture provides interest and variety.

Brennivín ('burnt wine'), nicknamed 'Black Death', is a strong schnapps distilled from potatoes and flavoured with caraway seeds.

Notorious nosh

Iceland's infamous traditional foods reflect the resourcefulness of its settlers. Rotten shark (*hákarl*) is buried for three months until rubbery and rotten, chopped into small cubes, and swilled down with schnapps. Guts, blood and fat, sewn up in a sheep's stomach, pressed, and pickled in whey, create haggis-like *slátur*. *Svið* are boiled and singed sheep's heads, eaten fresh or pickled. A real delicacy is *súrsaðir hrút-spungar* (pickled rams' testicles).

Less nightmarish are strips of *harðfiskur* (wind-dried cod or haddock) and *hangikjöt* (smoked lamb).

Food and drink prices

Price guide for a three-course meal for one, excluding wine:

$$$$ = over ISK10,000
$$$ = ISK5,000–10,000
$$ = ISK2,500–5,000
$ = below ISK2,500

The huldufólk of Icelandic folklore

SHOPPING

Icelandic products are perfect for those who appreciate quality and smart design – if your credit card can take the pain. Pick up weird food to amuse friends back home; or indulge in books, music, clothes and beautifully made homeware.

Shopping in Iceland is fun. Most shops in Reykjavík are small, one-off boutiques, packed with unusual, individualistic goodies that delight and amuse.

Icelandic design uses the clean lines and cool functionality of modernist Scandinavian products, but incorporates local materials, and is infused by a darker, quirkier spirit. The Iceland Design Centre (Aðalstræti 2; www.icelanddesign.is; Mon–Fri 9am–5pm) is an information centre where you can learn about Icelandic design and architecture. The centre also hosts events, exhibitions and conferences dedicated to local design.

On leaving Iceland, you can get a VAT (Value Added Tax) refund if you've spent over ISK6,000 in an eligible shop – see page 131.

WHERE TO BUY

Laugavegur is the main shopping street, with Hafnarstræti and Austurstræti also filled with outlets. Skólavörðustígur, branching diagonally off Laugavegur, is good for quirky gifts and crafts. Open at weekends, the city's flea market Kolaportið is fun to browse for half an hour – you never know what treasures you might find.

If you prefer chain stores, Kringlan (www.kringlan.is) is Iceland's largest shopping centre, with over 150 shops and food outlets, and is a 15-minute bus-ride from the city centre.

WHAT TO BUY

Art, design and homeware

Home to over 40 Icelandic designers, and offering everything from children's toys to ceramics, jewellery and clothes, Kraum (Hverfisgata 34 – enter from Laugavegur; www.facebook.com/kraum101) is a one-stop shop for cool homegrown design.

Kirsuberjatréð (Vesturgata 4; www.kirs.is) is a collective of 11 female artists selling weird and wonderful goods: fishskin handbags, bowls made from radishes and music boxes woven from feathers.

Skólavörðustígur contains a number of art galleries selling some excellent local work, as well as teeny-tiny shops with Icelandic ceramics, textiles, jewellery and graphic design.

Books

Iceland publishes more books per capita than any other country in the world, and Reykjavík's big bookshops – Eymundsson

Kraum design shop   *Nordic Store woollen jumpers*

(Austurstræti 18; Mon–Sat 9am–10pm, Sun 10am–10pm) and Mál og Menning (Laugavegur 18; Mon–Fri 9am–10pm, Sat–Sun 10am–10pm) – are delightful reflections of a literary nation. Both contain large English-language sections.

Clothes

Traditional woollen gloves, scarves, hats and the distinctive *lopapeysa* (sweater), with its colourful patterned yoke, are made from one-of-a-kind Icelandic sheep's wool. Beware of 'made in China' imposters: the Handknitting Association of Iceland (Handþrjónasamband Íslands; Skólavörðustigur 19; http://handknit.is; Mon–Sat 9am–6pm, Sun noon–6pm) sells the real deal, along with a rainbow array of wool if you want to knit your own. If you're travelling along the south coast to Vík, Víkurprjón (daily 8am–9pm) is a wool factory/shop where you can see garments being made.

Outdoor clothes companies Cintamani (http://cintamani.is), Icewear (www.icewear.is) and 66° North (www.66north.com) make tough, warm, stylish clothes, sold throughout Iceland, that keep the Icelandic weather out.

Lots of shops sell designer clothing, particularly for women, for example Kronkron (Laugavegur 63), or Kiosk (Ingólfsstræti 6), a collective of independent Icelandic designers.

Food and drink

Smoked salmon, roe caviar and dried fish are good buys, but be aware of any import restrictions. The confectionery shelves in supermarkets are packed with salted liquorice (*salmiak*), a typically Scandinavian passion. The powerful schnapps *brennivín*, with its minimalist black label, makes a good gift.

Music

Iceland is a nation full of musicians. Björk, Of Monsters and Men and Sigur Rós are the country's biggest musical exports, but the modern music scene is ever-changing and new bands appear all the time. Record-shop staff in Reykjavík are generally only too happy to help you through the overwhelming profusion of music: shops include independent label Smekkleysa (Laugavegur 35; https://smekkleysa.net), Reykjavík Record Shop (Klapparstígur 35; www.facebook.com/reykjavikrecordshop), 12 Tónar (Skólavörðustigur; www.12tonar.is) or Iceland's biggest record shop Lucky Records (Rauðarárstígur 10; http://lucky records.is).

For traditional Icelandic music, try the album *Íslensk alþýðulög* (Icelandic Folk Songs). There are also fine classical recordings by the Iceland Symphony Orchestra.

Skincare

The Blue Lagoon has a shop (Laugavegur 17; www.bluelagoon.com) in the city centre, where it sells its skincare line, which uses the minerals, silica mud and algae found in the lagoon's seawater. The products are especially good for people with dry skin or conditions such as psoriasis.

Reykjavík Culture Night is celebrated with a programme of free events around the city

ENTERTAINMENT

Reykjavík is well known for its weekend partying, when jolly drinkers pack the tiny bars. The city's harbourside concert hall, Harpa, is a measure of its ambition: a thriving cultural scene includes theatre, opera, ballet, orchestral performances and lively festivals.

Reykjavík used to be little more than a stopover en route to the main attractions: Iceland's spectacular glaciers, volcanoes, waterfalls, mountains and black beaches. But the city has been undergoing a transformation over the last 15 years. It's still small, but is now a city-break destination in its own right, with most of the country's entertainment concentrated here. There's a flourishing restaurant scene, a dazzling concert hall, bars and clubs with a quirky and vibrant nightlife, and plentiful gigs and festivals.

Icelanders have a passion for culture. What other city, with a population of a mere 120,000, has a symphony orchestra, two major professional theatre companies, numerous independent theatre groups, an opera company, a national dance company and both a national and municipal art gallery?

While local theatre excels (see page 125), most performances are in Icelandic and may prove inaccessible to visitors.

On top of this, dozens of smaller galleries and venues offer exhibitions, recitals and performances throughout the year, and an annual arts festival attracts artists of international standing. *What's On in Reykjavík*, a free monthly listing magazine, keeps track of it all, as does the free newspaper *The Reykjavík Grapevine* (www.grapevine.is).

MUSIC

Music is a rich part of Icelandic culture, particularly singing – even in the darkest days of the country's history, people could still raise up their voices. As Iceland was cut off for so long from the outside world, its traditional music has preserved characteristics that have been lost in other countries, such as the *hákveða* rhythm, and the chanted *rímur*, which date back to Viking times.

Pop music

Songs and music still permeate Icelandic culture today. Reykjavík's reputation as a 'happening' place largely grew out of the success of pop diva Björk, but she is just one of the country's many talented musicians – at times, it seems as though every Icelander plays an instrument or sings in a band. At weekends, many bars have live music, and the Iceland Airwaves (http://icelandairwaves.is) festival in November has an international reputation.

Rúntur – literally 'round tour' – refers to Reykjavík's weekend pub crawl

Classical music and opera

The city's sparkling, world-class concert hall, Harpa, was only halfway built when the country's economy collapsed in 2008. With banks folding left and right, still the money was found to complete this amazing edifice in 2011. It is home to both the Icelandic Opera and the internationally acclaimed Iceland Symphony Orchestra (ISO), who perform here from September to mid-June. The Opera is quite young, only dating back to the 1980s, but it is very popular with Icelandic audiences. It produces two to four operas every season, usually completely sold out. The ISO, currently led by French conductor Yan Pascal Tortelier, gives approximately 60 concerts every season. It has also produced 12 albums of music by Jón Leifs (1899–1968), perhaps Iceland's best-known composer.

NIGHTLIFE

Dozens of bohemian café-bars dot Laugavegur, Bankastræti, Hverfisgata and Austurstræti. They keep a low profile among the shops, serving coffee and cakes and the odd evening beer until the weekend comes, at which point the gloves come off. The pub crawl starts after midnight, when shouted conversations, flowing booze, live music and dancing become the Friday- and Saturday-night norm. People careen from bar to bar in a city-wide party, in search of the hottest sounds and coolest vibe.

On weekend nights, bars often stay open until 5am (1am during the week) and only tend to charge entrance fees if there's live music. Although most pubs are casual, people do get dressed up to go to smarter bars, and a few of the more exclusive places will turn you away if you're wearing jeans or trainers. Massive multi-floored nightclubs don't exist – the nightlife is on a small, intimate scale.

At closing time, the lights go on, but the action continues out in the street. If it's summer and the weather is good, everyone heads down to Lækjartorg square to mill around in a cheerful crowd or join the snaking queues at the hot-dog stalls.

The next morning, a late hangover-curing brunch is the traditional way of rounding the party off.

The Icelandic Dance Company

The Icelandic Dance Company (http://id.is/en) was founded as a classical ballet company in 1973. Part of the National Theatre of Iceland, the group turned its attention towards contemporary dance under the guidance of artistic director Katrín Hall, who took the reins in 1996. The Icelandic Dance Company functions as a national institution responsible for developing and cultivating contemporary dance and choreography. The group is Iceland's only professional dance company; it is well worth catching a show if you can.

Young climbers, Vestmannaeyjar islands

OUTDOOR ACTIVITIES

Iceland's wild landscapes offer a wealth of opportunities for all who love the great outdoors, whether you're splashing around in a mountain pool, rocking the waves on a whale-watching tour or exploring an ice cave in the dead of winter.

Iceland is an adventure holiday destination *par excellence*. Mountains, glaciers, lakes and thundering waterfalls are all here in abundance, with ever-increasing opportunities to enjoy them.

Everyone can get out into the countryside, whether on a short walk or a multi-day hike, on a bicycle or astride a gentle Icelandic horse. Naturalists are spoiled with epic bird cliffs and countrywide whale-watching opportunities; lovers of unearthly places can climb a glacier or explore an ice cave; and adrenaline junkies can hurtle down white-water rivers on a raft – just remember to look up once in a while at the staggering scenery.

EXPLORING THE COUNTRYSIDE

Walking and hiking
There are hiking trails throughout Iceland to suit every level. The best months for walking are June, July and August, when the weather is relatively warm, and visibility is at its best.

Ambitious routes into the unpopulated interior require previous experience, map and compass-reading abilities, good equipment and a high level of fitness. Always check weather conditions before setting off, go properly equipped and leave a travel plan with someone.

Two highly respected national outdoor organisations – Ferðafélag Íslands (FÍ; Iceland Touring Association; tel: 568 2533; www.fi.is) and Útivist (tel: 562 1000; www.utivist.is) – run guided day walks and backpacking trips, graded according to level of difficulty. They are extremely popular with Icelanders and book out quickly. Accommodation is usually in mountain huts, and participants must bring their own food and equipment.

Every part of the country has trails, including:

Þingvellir National Park. Gentle trails around historic sites and lakes. One option is a full-day hike up Mt Armannsfell.

Skaftafell (Vatnajökull National Park). Multi-level trails, from a well-trodden glacier path to the unmarked 24km (15-mile) round-trip to Kjós.

Mt Snæfell. A demanding 80km (50-mile) trail runs from Mt Snæfell to Stafafell, in the Lónsöræfi wilderness area.

Jökulsárgljúfur (Vatnajökull National Park). Well-marked trails at all levels, taking from a few hours to four days.

Lake Mývatn. Flat and gentle routes amid terrific scenery.

Spectacular cave in Vatnajökull ice cap

Hornstrandir. One of the wildest and most isolated parts of the country, suitable for the experienced only.

Snæfellsnes peninsula. Ascent to Snæfellsjökull glacier for experienced hikers.

Landmannalaugar–Þórsmörk Trail. The 53km (33-mile) 'Laugavegurinn' is Iceland's best-known hike, loved by experienced walkers.

Horse riding

Horses can go where even a jeep can't. Riding among deserted valleys and mountains, you gain real insight into the way Icelanders used to live. Icelandic horses are descended from the sturdy breed brought by the Vikings, and are famous for their unique fifth gait, the smooth tölt. Hey Iceland (www.heyiceland.is) lists farms that provide horse-riding tours and holidays, lasting from an hour to 10 days.

Make sure that your clothing is thoroughly washed and disinfected – Icelandic horses are not vaccinated and so are susceptible to disease brought from abroad.

Cycling

Unmade roads and high winds can make cycle touring a challenge. Two places with bikes for hire and pleasant cycling routes are Reykjavík and Lake Mývatn. In the capital, hire bicycles from Reykjavík Bike Tours (tel: 694 8956; http://icelandbike.com), who also offer a variety of guided summer bike tours, or Reykjavík Campsite (tel: 568 6944; www.reykjavikcampsite.is). The city has lots of good cycle paths, including one that runs around the edge of the peninsula.

For Lake Mývatn, see page 76.

The Icelandic Mountain Bike Club (Íslenski Fjallahjólaklúbburinn; tel: 562 0099; www.fjallahjolaklubburinn.is) is a great source of information for all cyclists.

NATURE WATCHING

Whale watching

Whale watching is a flourishing industry. Boats run year round, with a 90% cetacean-spotting success rate in summer, when migratory baleen whales swim north to feed, and calmer seas make it easier to see whales breaking the surface.

There are 23 species of cetaceans in Icelandic waters. You are most likely to see white-beaked dolphins, harbour porpoises, minke and humpbacks, or – if you're really lucky – sei, fin, blue, sperm and orca (killer) whales.

Húsavík is acknowledged as Iceland's 'whale-watching capital'. There are departures from other places on the north coast (Akureyri, Dalvík, Hauganes), the West Fjords (Holmavík), Snæfellsnes peninsula (Ólafsvík) and from Reykjavík. Choose an operator who abides by the IceWhale (http://icewhale.is) code of conduct.

Birdwatching

The prime birdwatching season is late April to early June, when staggering numbers – around 270 species – flock to their breeding sites. Puffins, gannets, gulls, guillemots and razorbills jostle for

space on the guano-spattered ledges of the world's largest seabird colonies.

Millions of birds can be found at Látrabjarg in the West Fjords, the largest bird cliff in Europe. Other big seabird colonies lie around Reykjanes peninsula, on Heimaey and at Dyrhólaey nature reserve. Heimaey was once the site of Iceland's largest puffin colony, although numbers are in sharp decline. Other puffin places include Lundey Island; around the cliffs at Vík; and at Borgarfjörður Eystri.

The great barren sandur on the south coast boast the world's largest skua colony; and clouds of crazed Arctic terns attack you pretty much everywhere.

Iceland's wetlands are packed with a wide array of waterfowl. Lake Mývatn has more species of breeding ducks than anywhere in Europe, including the colourful harlequin duck and Barrow's goldeneye.

Fuglavernd (BirdLife Iceland; http:// fuglavernd.is) protects and conserves Iceland's birds and habitats, and runs the Flói Bird Reserve near Eyrarbakki.

ICE AND SNOW

On the glaciers

Glacier walks: You can go for guided walks on most of Iceland's glaciers in summer, with the easiest taking around two hours. You need warm clothing and sturdy walking boots, but guides will provide you with ice axes, crampons and an explanation of glacier-walking techniques.

The Icelandic Mountain Guides (tel: 587 9999; www.mountainguides.is), Glacier Guides (tel: 659 7000, 571 2100; www.glacierguides.is) and Ice Guide (tel: 894 1317; www.localguide.is) take people onto Sólheimajökull, near Vík; Svínafellsjökull and Falljökul at Skaftafell; and Breiðamerkurjökull, by Jökulsárlón lagoon.

Ice caves and ice climbing: In winter, the three guiding companies offer trips to visit natural ice caves in Vatnajökull ice cap, as well as ice climbing and ambitious ascents of Iceland's highest peak Hvannadalshnúkur – see websites for details.

Dog-sledding: If there is enough snow, DogSledding Iceland (tel: 863 6733; www.dogsledding.is) run one-hour excursions on Langjökull glacier; otherwise you rattle along in a wheeled buggy, pulled over dry land by the dogs.

Snowmobiling: Several companies run snowmobile trips on Sólheimajökull, Snæfellsjökull and Langjökull, all of which can be arranged as day trips from Reykjavík – ask the tourist office for details.

Skiing

Iceland's ski slopes are not a holiday destination in their own right, but a popular diversion for Icelanders making the best of winter. Bláfjöll (tel: 530 3000; www.skidasvaedi.is), a 25-minute drive from Reykjavík, has 16 busy lifts and a café, open from mid-November to early May, depending on the snow. A day pass costs a very reasonable ISK3,550; boot and ski hire ISK5,000.

The best slopes are in northern Iceland at Akureyri (tel: 462 2280; www.hlidarfjall.is).

Crossing the virgin snow

INTO THE WATER

Swimming

Thanks to the country's lively geology, there is an abundance of naturally heated geothermal water, used to create swimming pools in towns and villages. There are over 120 municipal swimming baths, each with its own character and quirks, as well as naturally occurring hot springs, rivers and mountain pools – see https://sundlaugar.is for a full list.

As Icelandic pools are filled with constantly flowing water, chemical cleaners are rarely used. In order to keep the water as clean as possible, all swimmers must take a thorough shower in the nude before entering – which can come as something of a shock to the more bashful tourist.

White-water rafting

Visitors can shoot the rapids on three of Iceland's glacial rivers between May and mid-September. The fairly gentle Hvítá river is easily accessed on day trips from Reykjavík. However, if you're heading north, the remote Jökulsá Vestari and Jökulsá Austari, near Varmahlíð in Skagafjörður, should be your first choice. The western branch is suitable for families, while the eastern river is a wilder ride. For details, contact Arctic Rafting (tel: 562 7000; www.arcticrafting.com).

Snorkelling and scuba diving

A dry-suit qualification is required to be able to scuba dive in Iceland. Dive.is (tel: 578 6200; www.dive.is) offer the one-day PADI Dry Suit Course, plus daily diving and snorkelling tours to Silfra rift in Þingvellir National Park, as well as tours to other top-class dive sites around Iceland.

Kayaking

Hire kayaks to explore waterways and fjords in Stokkseyri, Seyðisfjörður and Ísafjörður; or Ice Guide (www.iceguide.is) can take you paddling on the tranquil Heinaberg glacial lagoon near Höfn.

Fishing

Salmon and trout fishing in Iceland have an international reputation: rivers must be booked months in advance. Permits are expensive, starting at around ISK40,000 per rod per day in peak season. The salmon season runs from 20 May to 30 September. Sea-run trout and char can be fished 1 April to 10 October; resident species can be fished year-round. For further information contact the Federation of Icelandic River Owners (tel: 563 0300; www.angling.is).

Arrange sea-angling trips directly through hotels and farms on the coast.

GAMES

Golf

Iceland has sixteen 18-hole courses; contact the Golf Federation of Iceland (Golfsamband Íslands; tel: 514 4050; www.golf.is, http://golficeland.org) for details. The major golfing event is the Arctic Open, held in June at Akureyri Golf Club (tel. 462 2974; www.arcticopen.is).

Sixteenth-century map of Iceland

HISTORY: KEY DATES

After an exciting Viking-packed start, Iceland suffered centuries of internal conflict, Danish oppression, deadly eruptions, famine, plague and pirate attacks. The 19th-century independence movement sowed the seeds for the modern republic we know today.

SETTLEMENT

500 or 600 AD	Irish monks settle on 'Thule'.
mid-9th century	Foiled by the harsh winter, would-be settler Hrafna-Flóki names the country Ísland (Iceland).
874	The 'First Settler' Ingólfur Arnarson makes his home in Reykjavík.
930	The Alþingi parliament is created.
10th century	Erik the Red leaves for Greenland; numerous Icelanders follow.

CONVERSION AND FEUDING

1000	Christianity adopted as Iceland's official religion.
1230–64	The Sturlung Age of violent conflicts between warring clans.
1262	The Alþingi allows King Haakon of Norway to collect taxes.

DISASTER AND DECLINE

1397	The Kalmar Union transfers sovereignty of Iceland from Norway to Denmark. Denmark establishes a trade monopoly, bringing terrible hardship; the monopoly lasts until 1854.
1402	The Black Death kills at least one-third of the population.
1550	Lutheran Reformation succeeds after the last Roman Catholic bishop, Jón Arason, is beheaded.
1783	Laki eruption and the ensuing 'Haze Famine' kill 10,000 Icelanders.
1800	Alþingi abolished by the Danish king; it is reinstated in 1843.

A REVIVAL OF FORTUNE

1801 and 1807	Two British naval victories over Denmark: the Danish navy is destroyed and the country's power declines.

Saga Museum tableau   *Eyjafjallajökull eruption of 2010*

1809	Jorgen Jorgensen, a Danish adventurer, 'liberates' Iceland – for two months.
1874	Denmark gives the Alþingi autonomy over domestic affairs, but retains a veto.

THE 20TH CENTURY AND BEYOND

1904	Iceland is granted home rule.
1918	Denmark makes Iceland a sovereign state, agreeing to negotiate further in 1940.
1940	With Iceland occupied by Britain and Denmark by Germany, there can be no negotiations. Alþingi takes over the governing of Iceland.
1944	Danish union terminated. On 17 June Iceland becomes a republic.
1949	Iceland becomes a founding member of NATO.
1952–76	Four Cod Wars (1952, 1958, 1972, 1975) with the UK over fishing rights.
1963	Surtsey island created by an underwater eruption.
1973	Eruption buries 400 houses on Heimaey; the island is evacuated.
1980	President Vigdís Finnbogadóttir becomes the world's first democratically elected female head of state.
1986	Ronald Reagan and Mikhail Gorbachev arrive in Reykjavík to discuss nuclear arms, a turning point in the Cold War.
1994	Iceland enters the European Economic Area.
2006	Iceland resumes commercial whaling, despite strong international opposition.
2008	Worldwide economic crisis hits Iceland; the major banks collapse, plunging the country into severe recession.
2009	Iceland applies for EU membership; the country suspends its application in 2013.
2010	Ash cloud from the Eyjafjallajökull eruption stops European air traffic for six days.
2016	Panama Papers reveal Iceland's Prime Minister Sigmundur Gunnlaugsson failed to declare ownership of an offshore company; PM resigns.
2017	Sexual abuse cover-up scandal brings the government down again. A new coalition is formed between the Left-Greens, the Independence Party and the Progressive Party, with Left-Green leader Katrin Jakobsdottir as PM.

BEST ROUTES

Enjoying the sunshine in Austurvöllur

CENTRAL REYKJAVÍK

The world's northernmost capital is a bright, colourful, friendly city. Rich in cultural attractions and with a vibrant nightlife, Reykjavík is also refreshingly small and green, with stunning glacier and mountain views, and whales swimming in Faxaflói Bay.

DISTANCE: 2.5km (1.5 miles)
TIME: A full day
START: Austurvöllur square
END: Laugavegur

Most visitors start and end their trip in **Reykjavík**, surrounded by whale-filled waves and bathed in northern light. Although over a third of Icelanders live here, the city retains a friendly, rustic feel that makes it unique among the world's capitals. There are few high-rise buildings, and the use of corrugated iron and timber makes many of its houses look almost temporary.

Major roads wrap around the edge of town, but in the centre the streets are narrow and pedestrian-friendly. Cafés, bars, live music, art galleries, little museums and interesting one-off boutiques thrive. Everything is either within walking distance or a short cycle, bus or taxi ride away.

For a visitor, the old city centre is the most charming part of the capital. Residential streets, with brightly coloured corrugated-iron houses, abut the shops, cafés and galleries of the main thoroughfares.

AUSTURVÖLLUR

The heart of the city is **Austurvöllur** ❶ ('eastern field'), a small grassy square where the Viking First Settler Ingólfur Arnarson grew his hay. It may not look like much, but it is rich with symbols of nationhood. At its centre is a **statue of Jón Sigurðsson**, leader of the independence movement, who fought to free Iceland from Danish control.

Jón gazes at the **Parliament Building** ❷ (Alþingishúsið), a well-proportioned basalt mansion built in 1880−81 to house the ancient assembly. Today, the headquarters of the Icelandic parliament accommodates the country's 63 MPs. When parliament is sitting, debates can be observed from the public gallery; but they are, of course, in Icelandic. Archaeological digs around the building unearthed the first Viking Age industrial site found in Iceland: an iron smithy and fish- and wool-processing facilities.

Next door to Alþingishúsið is Reykjavík's neat white **Lutheran cathedral** ❸ (Dómkirkjan; http://domkirkjan. is; Mon−Fri 10am−4pm; free), built in

National Gallery of Iceland

1785. Its trim, galleried interior has a ceiling studded with golden stars.

AROUND TJÖRNIN

Slip between the parliament and the cathedral to behold the lovely city-centre lake **Tjörnin** ❹ ('The Pond'), favoured by around 40 species of birds, most noticeably ducks. On its northern bank is **Reykjavík City Hall** ❺ (Raðhús), a key example of 20th-century Icelandic architecture. The modern glass-and-concrete construction contains a café, a large 3D map of Iceland and the main **Visit Reykjavík tourist office** (tel: 411 6040; www. visitreykjavik.is; daily 8am–8pm).

Viking history

Turn left on Vonarstræti, then right down Tjarnargata, to **Aðalstræti**, the city's oldest street. The **Reykjavík 871±2 Settlement Exhibition** ❻ (Landnámssýning; Aðalstræti 16; www.reykjavik871.is; daily 9am–6pm) does an impressive and imaginative job of exploring how it might have been in Viking times. The underground museum is built around the remains of an excavated Viking Age farmhouse. A modest-looking turf wall belonging to the farm presents a tantalising puzzle: it lies underneath a layer of volcanic ash dated to AD 871... three years before the official settlement date.

For a wider exploration of Iceland's history, walk back down Tjarnargata, admiring the swans and other birdlife on The Pond, before crossing the busy Ring Road to the excellent **National Museum of Iceland** ❼ (Þjoðminjasafn Íslands; Hringbraut, Suðurgata 1, junction with Hringbraut; www.thjodmin jasafn.is; May–mid-Sept daily 10am–5pm, mid-Sept–Apr Tue–Sun 10am–5pm). The museum's main exhibition, *The Making of a Nation*, is gripping stuff, tracing Iceland's history from the Viking settlement to the present day. The section on the use of DNA testing is particularly interesting, detailing work done on the teeth of the first settlers to determine their origins. Allow a couple of hours, then stop for a light lunch at the museum café, **Kaffitár**, see ❶.

Listasafn Íslands

Head back along Tjarnargata, turning right on Skothúsvegur, which crosses the lake. On the other side is the **National Gallery of Iceland** ❽ (Listasafn Íslands; Fríkirkjuvegur 7; www.listasafn.is; mid-May–mid-Sept daily 10am–5pm, rest of the year Tue–Sun 11am–5pm), originally built as an ice house to store blocks cut from Tjörnin. The gallery is small, but has a fine permanent collection of work by Icelandic artists, including the country's first professional painter Ásgrímur Jónsson (1876–1958).

FRÍKIRKJUVEGUR AND LÆKJARGATA

Walk north along Fríkirkjuvegur, which becomes Lækjargata. The imposing white building at the top of the grassy

Restaurants on Laugavegur

bank to your right is the grammar school **Menntaskólinn í Reykjavík ❾**, noteworthy enough to appear on the 500-krónur banknote.

Follow Skólabrú, the street opposite the school, back to the corner of Austurvöllur. **Hotel Borg ❿**, the city's first hotel, was built in 1930 by a circus strongman, and fills the eastern side of the square. Walk alongside it down Pósthússtræti.

LÆKJARTORG AND BANKASTRÆTI

When you reach the main post office, look to your left and right. The streets stretching in either direction – Austurstræti, Bankastræti and Laugavegur – contain a plethora of pubs and restaurants that lend a buzzing atmosphere to downtown Reykjavík at night. Turn right, passing **Lækjartorg ⓫**, a traditional meeting-place, and cross dual-laned Lækjargata.

At the western end of Bankastræti, on your left is **Government House ⓬** (Stjórnarráðshúsið; not open to the public), one of the oldest buildings in the country. Originally built in 1761 as a prison, it now houses the offices of the Prime Minister. On your right, down the stairs of an old public toilet, is the tiny **Icelandic Punk Museum ⓭** (Pönksafns Íslands; http://thepunkmuseum.is; Mon–Fri 10am–10pm, Sat–Sun noon–10pm), a project of passion where you can listen to music, play bass, guitar

and drums, and learn about the history of punk in Iceland.

Take a quick detour left down Ingólfsstræti. Across Hverfisgata, standing on a hillock, is an imposing **statue of**

Serving Icelandic hot dogs　　　　　*A trendy Reykjavík shop*

Ingólfur Arnarson ⓮, the First Settler, who appears to be admiring the glinting Snæfellsjökull ice cap, 100km (62 miles) away. Behind him is the **Culture House** ⓯ (Þjóðmenningarhúsið; Hverfisgata 15; www.culturehouse.is; May–mid-Sept daily 10am–5pm, mid-Sept–Apr Tue–Sun 10am–5pm), a must for anyone interested in the sagas. Its fascinating medieval manuscripts are full of details of life in

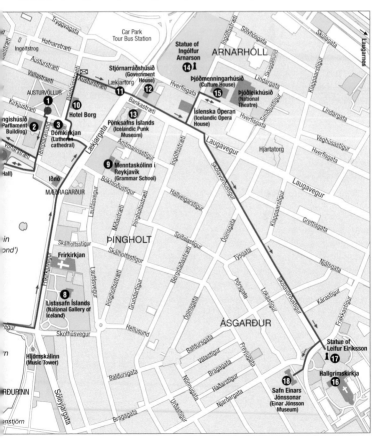

Arresting Hallgrímskirkja

Iceland and northern Europe from the time of the Vikings onwards. The splendid building, opened in 1909, was initially intended to be the National Library.

LAUGAVEGUR AND SKÓLAVÖRÐUSTÍGUR

Bankastræti quickly becomes **Laugavegur**, the city's main shopping street, full of cafés, restaurants, bars, hotels and lovely boutiques. Laugavegur translates literally as 'Hot Spring Road' – it was once the path taken by townspeople when they went to do their washing in the hot pools in Laugardalur (see page 40).

Branch diagonally right onto **Skólavörðustígur**. As you head uphill, admire the enticing galleries and bijoux boutiques, reflecting on how much artistic talent such a small country has produced... that is, if you can tear your eyes away from massive **Hallgrímskirkja** 🟤 (www.hallgrimskirkja.is; daily May–Sept 9am–9pm, Oct–Apr 9am–5pm; free, but charge for tower), soaring like a rocket at the top end of the street. Designed by Guðjón Samúelsson, this modern concrete church was built in nationalistic style to resemble volcanic basalt columns, and is a monument not only to God, but also to Iceland's belief that even a small country can have big dreams.

The message is reinforced by a statue outside of **Leifur Eiríksson** 🟤, Iceland's greatest adventurer, who reached America long before Christopher Columbus. The statue, by Alexander Stirling Calder, was a gift from the US government to mark the Icelandic parliament's 1,000th anniversary in 1930.

Inside, the church is plainly and soberly Lutheran, except for the extravagant organ, which is 15 metres (50ft) high and has more than 5,000 pipes. A lift runs up Hallgrímskirkja's 73-metre (240ft) tower – with a few stairs at the end – from where you are rewarded with great views of Reykjavík from the viewing platform.

If time is getting short, you might want to visit the neighbouring museum before the church. The **Einar Jónsson Museum** 🟤 (Safn Einars Jónssonar; Njarðargata; www.lej.is; Tue–Sun 10am–5pm) is the former home and studio of sculptor Einar Jónsson (1874–1954), a master of symbolism. Jónsson was virtually a recluse towards the end of his life, and many of the 100 or so pieces exhibited here are very melancholy in character. At the back of the building, on Freyjugata, the small sculpture garden is open year-round.

Head back to Laugavegur for your pick of the city's restaurants for dinner.

Food and drink

🍴 KAFFITÁR

National Museum of Iceland; tel: 530 2201; www.thjodminjasafn.is; 9am–5pm May–mid-Sept Mon–Fri, mid-Sept–Apr Tue–Fri, Sat–Sun 10am–5pm year round; $
This bright museum café offers a range of coffee, soups, salads and local delicacies.

Kolaportið Flea Market

Sculptures by Ásmundur Sveinsson

REYKJAVÍK HARBOURS

The streets around Reykjavík's old and new harboursides are packed with excellent museums and galleries, cafés and restaurants. Whale- and bird-watching trips also depart from here; seeing whales, dolphins and colourful puffins in their natural habitat is unforgettable.

DISTANCE: 2km (1.25 miles)
TIME: 1 day
START: Hafnarstræti
END: Ægisgarður
POINTS TO NOTE: This tour includes whale-watching – book an evening trip to leave time for daytime sight-seeing.

Reykjavík's waterfront has been moved and developed over the years, leaving both old and new harboursides to explore.

HAFNARSTRÆTI

As its name suggests, **Hafnarstræti** ('harbour street') was once the old quayside. During World War I, the land was extended by dumping gravel and sand in the sea to form Tryggvagata; Tryggvagata was extended again into today's harbourfront Geirsgata. Hafnarstræti contains some of the city's oldest buildings, such as **Fálkahúsið ❶** (Nos 1–3), where the king of Denmark kept his prize falcons: two carved wooden birds on the roof commemorate the fact.

TRYGGVAGATA

On Tryggvagata, from east to west, are Kolaportið, Hafnarhús, the library and Volcano House, all of interest to visitors. **Kolaportið Flea Market ❷** (Tryggvagata 19; www.kolaportid.is; Sat–Sun 11am–5pm) is small but cheerful, selling second-hand clothes, books and odds and ends. The food section is a must for anyone curious about traditional fishy treats, like *harðfiskur* (dried fish), *hákarl* (cured shark) and *síld* (pickled herring).

Reykjavík Art Museum: Hafnarhús ❸ (Listasafn Reykjavíkur: Hafnarhús; Tryggvagata 17; http://artmuseum.is/hafnarhus; daily 10am–5pm, Thu until 10pm), one of three galleries belonging to the Reykjavík Art Museum, is situated in the stylishly renovated former warehouse of the Port of Reykjavík. Here you will find changing contemporary art exhibitions, as well as permanent works by internationally renowned Icelandic pop artist, Erró (1932–).

Next door, the **city library** (Borgarbókasafn Reykjavíkur) has an interesting little **photo museum ❹**

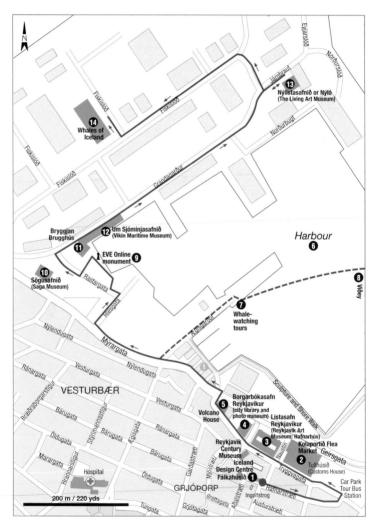

Lonely Viðey Island

(Tryggvagata 15; www.ljosmyndasafn reykjavikur.is; Mon–Fri 11am–6pm, Sat–Sun 1–5pm) on the top floor, with changing exhibitions showing off some of the six million photographs in its collection.

A couple of blocks away, a very different kind of visual experience awaits at **Volcano House** ❺ (Tryggvagata 11; www.volcanohouse.is; daily 9am–10pm, shows on the hour 10am–9pm). Two films (screened together; run-time 53 minutes) show dramatic footage of the 1973 Heimaey eruption and the 2010 Eyjafjallajökull eruption, supported by an exhibition on Iceland's unique geology.

Cross busy Geirsgata and turn left towards the harbour. A cluster of teal-coloured buildings on the right offer a host of tasty lunch options, such as **Höfnin** (see ❶).

BOAT TRIPS FROM ÆGISGARÐUR

The modern **harbour** ❻ is still operational, with fishing boats bringing in their catch. The highly controversial **whaling ships** are recognisable by their black hulls and a red H (for 'hvalur') on their funnels.

Wildlife tours

If you turn right on Ægisgarður, three companies offer much more conservation-friendly 2.5–3-hour **whale-watching tours** ❼ in Faxaflói, the bay which lies between the capital and the Snæfellsnes peninsula – **Elding** (tel: 519 5000; www.elding.is), **Special Tours** (tel: 560 8800; www.specialtours.is) and **Whale Safari** (tel: 497 0000; www.whalesafari.is). Minke whales, white-beaked dolphins and harbour porpoises are most commonly spotted here, but fin, blue, sei, humpback, sperm and killer whales are also possible sightings. Boats sail past the tiny island of **Lundey** between mid-May and mid-August, so passengers can get a good look at the **puffins**. There's still lots to see at the harbour, so if possible return for an evening tour (7pm/8.30pm/9pm between June and August, depending on the company).

Viðey island

In summertime, Elding also runs the ferry (tel: 533 5055; mid-May and August at hourly intervals from Ægisgarður pier; year-round departures from Skarfabakki pier) to the island of **Viðey** ❽, a haunting and historically significant place full of tussocked grass and soughing wind. The bird life is prolific, and there are some impressive basalt columns on the isthmus at the centre of the island, as well as modern sculptures including Yoko Ono's *Imagine Peace Tower*, which lights up the sky on significant dates. In contrast, its church is the oldest in the country, dating from 1774. The ferry takes less than 10 minutes, and Viðey is small enough to stroll around in an hour or two.

GRANDI HARBOUR

Geirsgata now changes its name to Mýrargata. Continue west, following the pedestrian path, painted with blue and yellow stripes, to the **EVE Online monument** ❾. Covered in the names of hundreds of thousands of players, the monument celebrates the 10th anniversary of one of Iceland's most successful exports, a massive online sci-fi game.

The path pops out on Grandagarður, an up-and-coming area of the city: over the past five years, trendy shops, bistros and studios have been springing up along its length. On your left is the **Saga Museum** ❿ (Sögusafnið; www.sagamuseum.is; daily 10am–6pm), Iceland's equivalent of Madame Tussauds. Dramatic tableaux with life-size models of saga characters bring the country's medieval history to life.

On your right is **Bryggjan Brugghús** ⓫ (http://bryggjanbrugghus.is; daily 11am–1am), Iceland's first microbrewery, with a popular bistro and a **beer school** (tel: 456 4040; in English daily 5pm) where you can have an hour-long tasting session.

Next door, **Vikin Maritime Museum** ⓬ (Um Sjóminjasafnið; daily 10am–5pm) explores Iceland's fishing industry, including the three notorious 'Cod Wars' with Britain. There are guided tours aboard the coastguard ship Óðinn every day at 1pm, 2pm and 3pm.

Right at the end of the street, at No 20, is **The Living Art Museum** ⓭ (Nýlistasafnið or Nýló; www.nylo.is; Tue–Sun noon–6pm, Thu until 9pm; free), an artist-run not-for-profit art gallery with six to eight different contemporary exhibitions every year.

Curl back round on Fiskislóð to **Whales of Iceland** ⓮ (http://whalesoficeland.is; daily 10am–5pm) to learn about these amazing creatures. Whalesong accompanies you through this multimedia exhibition, lit as though underwater and containing 23 life-size models of the various whale species around Iceland's coast. There's an audio app and virtual reality glasses to round off the experience.

Eat dinner in one of the many fabulous harbourside restaurants, returning to Ægisgarður for your evening whale-watching trip.

Food and drink

❶ HÖFNIN

Geirsgata 7c; www.hofnin.is; tel: 511 2300; daily 11:30am–10pm; $$$

One of several excellent eating options, set in the teal-coloured warehouses by the harbour. It would be churlish to eat anything except for the catch of the day at this cosy seafood restaurant. Ask for a window seat, with fabulous sea views.

Jón Gunnar Árnason's 'Sólfar 34' sculpture pays homage to Iceland's Viking history

REYKJAVÍK BIKE TOUR

A fabulous, smooth walking and cycle path hugs Reykjavík and runs around almost the whole Seltjarnarnes peninsula, with mesmerising views – perfect for exploring some hidden gems that lie a little further afield.

DISTANCE: 20km (12 miles)
TIME: 1 day
START: Reykjavík Bike Tours, Ægisgarður
END: Grótta lighthouse
POINTS TO NOTE: This route is a cycle ride on the excellent coastal path, but you could also see the major sights by bus or taxi; a private shuttle bus runs directly between Harpa and Perlan. Pack a swimsuit for the beach at Nauthólsvík.

You can hire a bicycle from **Reykjavík Bike Tours ❶** (Ægisgarður 7; tel: 694 8956; http://icelandbike.com; May–Sept daily 9am–5pm, by arrangement at other times), near the whale-watching companies at the harbour. The outlined route is around 20km (12 miles) long – flat and very easy with good-quality bikes.

THE NORTH COAST

From Ægisgarður, follow the pedestrianised path (sometimes called the 'Sculpture and Shore Walk') east to **Harpa ❷**

(tel: 528 5000; http://en.harpa.is; building daily 8am–midnight, box office Mon–Fri 9am–6pm, Sat–Sun 10am–6pm). The award-winning concert hall's glittering exterior, designed by artist Ólafur Elíasson, reflects the sea and sky in a kaleidoscopic lightshow. Inside it has four concert halls with state-of-the-art acoustic technology, which can be adjusted according to the type of music being played. From mid-June to August, there are 30-minute guided **tours** of the building on the hour (daily 10am to 5pm; less frequently at other times).

400 metres/yds east is Jón Gunnar Árnason's stunning sculpture *Sólfar 34 ❸* (*Sun Voyager*; 1986), based on a classic Viking longboat.

Detour up Snorrabraut

You might want to interrupt the cycle along the idyllic coastal path by turning right up Snorrabraut to the **Icelandic Phallological Museum ❹** (Hið Íslenzka Reðasafn; Laugavegur 116; http://phallus.is; daily 10am–6pm), displaying over 200 penises from almost every Icelandic mammal, including a 95-year-

Botanical Gardens

old human who bequeathed his member to the museum. A little further inland is the **Municipal Gallery** ❺ (Listasafn Reykjavíkur: Kjarvalsstaðir; Flókagata; http://artmuseum.is/kjarvalsstadir; daily 10am–5pm). Half the gallery is dedicated to the huge, colourful, often abstract landscapes by Icelandic artist Jóhannes Kjarval (1885–1972), while the other half houses visiting exhibitions.

Towards the cruise-ship harbour

Otherwise continue on the coast to **Höfði House** ❻ (closed to the public), isolated on a grassy square. Höfði was the location for the summit meetings in 1986 between President Reagan and Soviet leader Mikhail Gorbachev to discuss global disarmament.

One more kilometre east, just off the cycle path, is a peaceful art museum with awkward opening hours – you could return for one of its summer music recitals at 8.30pm on Tuesdays. **Sigurjón Ólafsson Museum** ❼ (Listasafn Sigurjóns Ólafssonar; Laugarnestangi 70; http://lso.is; June–mid-Sept Tue–Sun 2–5pm, mid Sept–Nov and Feb–May Sat–Sun 2–5pm) is dedicated to an Icelandic painter who lived from 1908 to 1982. In addition to the art collection, there is a small family-run café with a lovely sea view.

You get a second chance to sail to **Viðey** (see page 37) from Skarfabakki wharf at Sundahöfn harbour, just east of the museum, where the cruise ships dock.

LAUGARDALUR

Otherwise turn inland along Kirkjusandur and Laugalækur to **Laugardalur** ❽,

Höfði House, built in 1909

a green valley that serves as the capital's sports and recreation area, with an open-air swimming pool, camping ground, football stadium and sports hall. The **Botanical Gardens** ❾ (Grasagarður Reykjavíkur; www.grasagardur.is; daily May–Sept 10am–10pm, Oct–Apr 10am–3pm; free) have an impressive

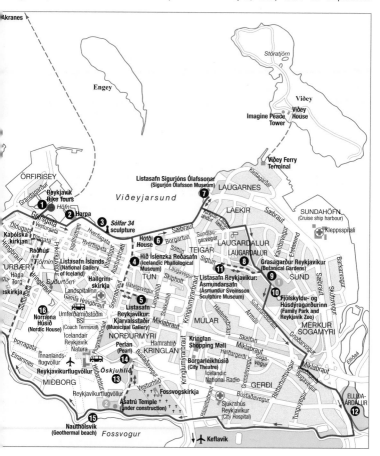

Perlan café

collection of 5,000 plants, and a summer café, **Flóran** (see ①). There are also Viking-themed mini-rides at the **Family Park and Reykjavík Zoo ⑩** (Fjölskyldu- og Húsdýragarðurinn; www.mu.is; daily 10am–5pm, until 6pm in summer), which contains domestic farm animals, Arctic foxes, mink, reindeer, seals and a small cold-water aquarium.

On the edge of Laugardalur is **Ásmundur Sveinsson Sculpture Museum ⑪** (Listasafn Reykjavíkur: Ásmundarsafn; Sigtún 105; http://artmuseum.is/asmundarsafn; daily May–Sept 10am–5pm, Oct–Apr 1–5pm). This is modern sculpture at its best, with huge figures depicting the people of Iceland as well as mythical characters.

Pass right through Laugardalur, popping out at the southwest corner on Engjavegur.

ELLIÐAÁRDALUR VALLEY

From here, you could cut straight across the peninsula, but the next 5km (3-mile) stretch is not much longer and takes you along quiet paths and into Elliðaárdalur valley before joining the southern coast.

Turn left onto the path running alongside busy Suðurlandsbraut, following it for 1km (0.5 miles) as it curves to the right, crossing Miklabraut over a pedestrian bridge, then turning immediately left on the cycle path. The path runs south alongside a major road before diving underneath it through a tunnel into the pretty wooded valley of **Elliðaárd-**

alur ⑫ – follow it to the right, where it goes back under the road after 400 metres/yds and heads due west. It travels through the Fossvogur district, past relaxing green spaces – football pitches, fields, Fossvogsdalur park, allotments – before crossing the Ring Road by bridge and becoming a coastal path once more.

ÖSKJUHLÍÐ AND PERLAN

Seven hundred metres (0.5 miles) beyond the footbridge, you can take another detour inland, turning right up **Öskjuhlíð ⑬** hill, green and leafy thanks to tree-planting schemes. The path passes a building site where an Ásatrú (pagan Norse) temple is being constructed, rising to the glass-domed **Perlan ⑭** ('Pearl'). This extraordinary building is actually six enormous tanks that store the city's hot water supply – 24 million litres (over 5 million gallons) of geothermally heated water. Inside, a revolving restaurant sits atop the tanks; below is a **360° viewing deck** with super views; and on the ground floor is the brand-new **Perlan Museum** (www.perlanmuseum.is; daily 9am–7pm). So far there is one exhibition about Iceland's glaciers, which includes a man-made ice cave; but two others – on the geology of Iceland and a planetarium – are due to open in 2018.

THE SOUTH COAST

Sticking to the coast will bring you to another little jewel – Reykjavík's

Nauthólsvík beach *Grótta lighthouse, inaccessible at high tide*

purpose-built geothermal beach at **Nauthólsvík** **⑮** (www.nautholsvik. is; mid-May–mid-Aug daily 10am–7pm, mid Aug–mid-May Mon and Wed 11am–2pm and 5–8pm, Fri 11am–2pm, Sat 11am–4pm; free). This little crescent of golden sand is a slice of happiness on a sunny day, when people flock here to catch the rays and bathe outdoors in the heated bay. The seawater reaches 20°C (68°F), and there is a geothermal hot pot that gets even hotter (up to 35°C/95°F). Stop for coffee and cake at the café-bistro **Nauthóll** (see **②**) before continuing along the coast.

SHORTCUT HOME

If you're tired, you can start heading across the peninsula for home, 2km (1.2 miles) away, just past the domestic airport. As you pass the very western end of the east–west runway, turn off onto Suðurgata, follow it to its end, turn left onto Túngata, then right onto Ægisgata by the Catholic church – this will lead you back to the bike shop. On the way, look out for **Nordic House** **⑯** (Norræna Húsið; Sturlugata; www.nordichouse.is; exhibition space daily 11am–5pm; free except for some exhibitions), designed by the renowned Finnish architect Alvar Aalto. Its purpose is to cultivate and strengthen ties between the Nordic countries. It contains a library, design shop and a good upmarket 'New Nordic' restaurant, and has an ongoing programme of exhibitions and concerts.

SELTJARNARNES PENINSULA

If you still have spring in your saddle, you can follow the coastal path all the way around the peninsula back to the bike shop, a distance of about 8km (5 miles). This takes you around the headland of Seltjarnarnes, a beautiful little spot with a real feeling of wildness, despite being so close to the city. Pass the golf club and Bakkatjörn lake, before reaching the path to **Grótta lighthouse** **⑰** (closed May to June due to bird nesting), from where you can watch the seabirds and the waves that come pounding in from the Atlantic. Keep an eye on the tides, though, otherwise you could get stranded!

Food and drink

① FLÓRAN

Botanical Gardens, Laugardalur; tel: 553 8872; www.floran.is; May–Sept daily 10am–10pm; $$$

A Scandinavian bistro with a strong Danish influence, this tranquil place grows many of the ingredients in its own greenhouses, and makes its own lemonade. Weekend brunch (11am–3pm) is particularly popular.

② NAUTHÓLL

Nauthólsvegur 106; www.nautholl.is; tel: 599 6660; daily 11am–10pm; $$$

If you're visiting Perlan or Nauthólsvík beach, make a stop at this classy bistro, splashed with sea light and full of scrummy morsels.

The steamy Blue Lagoon

REYKJANES

Jutting out into the sea southwest of the capital, the Reykjanes peninsula is an otherworldly landscape of moss-topped lava fields and wild rocky shores. The undisputed highlight is the world-famous Blue Lagoon, but there are also excellent bird-watching sites and nature reserves.

DISTANCE: 118km (73 miles)
TIME: A full day
START: Viking World, Njarðvík
END POINT: Hafnarfjörður
POINTS TO NOTE: Prebook your ticket and pack your swimsuit for the Blue Lagoon. A descent into the Þríhnúkagígur volcano is best done as a separate six-hour trip from Reykjavík. Although we have outlined this tour as a one-day driving route, the flatness of the peninsula makes it a popular two-day cycling route.

Ninety-nine percent of visitors to Iceland first set foot on the Reykjanes peninsula – Keflavík International Airport sits at its furthest edge. But apart from spending a few dallying hours at the Blue Lagoon, most people head onwards to Reykjavík without a backward glance.

However, this region rewards those who look beyond the apparent stillness and emptiness. Reykjanes is one of the most volatile areas of the country, a Unesco Global Geopark (www.reykjanes geopark.is) with 55 separate sites of interest, including lava flows, fissures, craters, shield volcanoes, steam vents and bubbling mud pools. Busy fisher-men haul in boats at tiny villages, while the low cliffs are packed with millions of squawking seabirds.

THE NORTHWESTERN TIP

Near the airport

You can get an early start to the day's sight-seeing trip by starting at **Viking World ❶** (Víkingabraut 1; tel: 422 2000; www.vikingworld.is; daily 7am–6pm) in Njarðvík. The dramatic modern glass building contains the replica Viking ship *Íslendingur*, and four exhibitions about Norse exploration and the settlement of Iceland.

Follow the main road Njarðarbraut northwest around the bay to **Keflavík ❷**, which used to house a large American air base. The base's closure in 2006 had an unsettling effect on the area, although it is slowly regenerating. Continue as the road changes to sculpture-dotted Hafnargata, then Duusgata, stopping at the **Duus Museum Cultural**

Space-like Reykjanes Geopark

Centre (Duusgata 2–8; tel: 421 3245; www.duusmuseum.is; summer Mon–Fri 9am–5pm, Sat–Sun noon–5pm, rest of year daily noon–5pm), a cluster of historic harbourside buildings. Inside are the **regional tourist information centre** (www.visitreykjanes.is) and **Geopark visitor centre** (www.reykjanesgeopark. is), plus eight exhibition halls housing collections of art, model boats and history. At the very end, **Kaffi Duus** (see ①) makes a good morning coffee stop.

Miðnes

Join the Ring Road heading northwest, then turn right onto Route 45. Beyond Keflavík is the outcrop known as **Miðnes** ❸, where the biggest settlements are the tiny fishing outposts of **Garður** (hometown of the lead singer of Of Monsters and Men) and **Sandgerði**. Drive through Garður, turning right onto Route 402 and following 'Garðsskagaviti' signs to the windswept headland **Garðskagi** ❹, with two lighthouses, a café and a

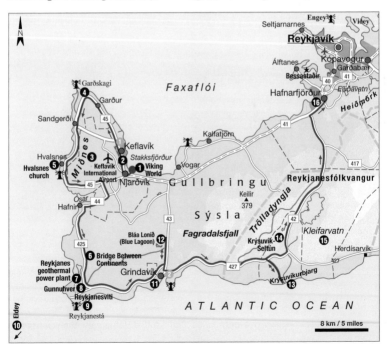

Inside Þríhnúkagígur volcano

little folk museum, a fantastic place for birdwatching and spotting whales.

From Garðskagi, head due south on Route 45 through bleak flat plains of lava, edged by the ocean, passing through Sandgerði to **Hvalsnes church** ❺, built from bits of basalt and driftwood in 1887. There's also a gravestone handcut by poet Reverend Hallgrímur Péturssonin in 1649. The ruins of the village **Bátsendar** are a little to the south, destroyed by a freak tide at the end of the 18th century.

Follow Route 45 to its end at a T-junction, and turn right onto Route 44/425, which follows the coast down to the peninsula's southwestern tip.

SOUTHWARDS DOWN THE COAST

After 12km (7.5 miles), stop for a photo opportunity at the **Bridge Between Continents** ❻. A footbridge spans the rift between the North American and Eurasian tectonic plates, a graphic illustration of the boundary where the earth's crust rips itself in two at the rate of around 2cm (0.75ins) each year.

A scant kilometre beyond the shining silver **Reykjanes geothermal power plant** ❼, take a quick detour west to see the smoking yellow hot-spring area **Gunnuhver** ❽, named after an angry ghost who haunts the area, and Iceland's oldest and most beloved lighthouse, **Reykjanesviti** ❾. If you look out to sea, you'll see the sheer-sided island of **Eldey** ❿, 14km (9 miles) offshore. Eldey is home to one of the North Atlantic's largest gan-

net colonies – around 16,000 pairs nest on the island each year. The island is a fiercely protected nature reserve, with access forbidden to casual visitors. It is also the place where the last of the great auks was clubbed to death in 1844.

GRINDAVÍK

Route 425 brings you to **Grindavík** ⓫, a refreshingly workaday fishing community of about 3,200 people with a long and eventful history. It was a major trading centre during the Middle Ages, and in 1532 a business rivalry between English and Hanseatic merchants led to the murder of an Englishman, John 'the Broad'. Barbary pirates raided Grindavík in 1627, abducting several dozen captives who were then sold as slaves in Africa.

Two keystones of Iceland's survival – saltfish and geothermal energy – are celebrated at the **Kvikan House of Culture & Natural Resources** (Kvikan auðlinda-og menningarhús; Hafnargata 12a; tel: 420 1190; www.grindavik.is/kvikan; May 14–Aug 31 daily 10am–5pm, rest of the year Sat–Sun 11am–5pm). Stop for lunch at the saltfish restaurant **Salthúsið** (see ❷) before heading for the Blue Lagoon, just 4km (2.5 miles) away.

THE BLUE LAGOON

Iceland's most famous tourist attraction, the **Blue Lagoon** ⓬ (Bláa Lonið; tel: 420 8800; www.bluelagoon.com; daily July–mid-Aug 7am–midnight, June

Turquoise waters meet black sands

7am–11pm, Jan–May and mid-Aug–Sept 8am–10pm, Oct–Dec 8am–9pm), is a dreamy, steamy spa complex that epitomises the country's faintly unearthly reputation. Little wooden bridges criss-cross its blue-white waters, which are a toasty 37–40°C (98–104°F) all year round. The complex – being expanded in 2018 – also contains a spa treatment area, restaurant, snack bar, shop and guesthouse.

In spite of its evocative name, the lagoon is not a natural phenomenon but a fortuitous by-product of Iceland's geothermal energy usage. The nearby Svartsengi power plant pumps up superheated saltwater from 2km (1.25 miles) underground. This water is used to generate electricity and heat fresh water, after which it flows into the lagoon. Rich in silica, salt and other minerals, the run-off is great for your skin!

Due to overwhelming visitor numbers, you must now prebook online. Although you must turn up as booked, you can stay as long as you like. People spend an average of two hours bathing in the balmy waters.

KRÝSUVÍK AND KLEIFARVATN

Take Route 427 east out of Grindavík. After 16km (10 miles), ornithologists or walkers might want to investigate **Krýsuvíkurbjarg** ⓭, one of Iceland's best-known bird-cliffs. A rough jeep track is signposted to the right, but unless you have a 4WD, it's better to park off the main road and take a 40-minute walk down to the cliffs. The most numerous inhabitants are kittiwakes, with fulmar, razorbill, common guillemot and Brunnich's guillemot also plentiful. Seals bask in the rocky coves, and you might glimpse pods of whales offshore.

Four kilometres (2.5 miles) further along Route 427, turn north onto Route 42, signposted to Krýsuvík. A well-maintained boardwalk winds through the bubbling, belching, hissing **Krýsuvík-Seltún** ⓮ geothermal area. Sulphur deposits, once in demand for making gunpowder, give the boiling mud springs and *solfataras* their

---

Þríhnúkagígur volcano

Many tourist attractions are touted as once-in-a-lifetime experiences. In the case of Iceland's Þríhnúkagígur volcano (May–Sept), it's completely true. This volcano is the only one in the world with an empty, intact, multicoloured magma chamber into which visitors can descend – via a window cleaners' platform. The chamber is big enough to fit the Statue of Liberty, with room to spare.

The volcano is dormant, last erupting more than 4,000 years ago. Its chamber was discovered in 1974 by Árni B. Stefánsson, a veteran cave explorer, and opened to visitors in 2012.

Although the volcano is relatively close to Kleifarvatn, the roads are rough and slow. It's easiest to use the Inside the Volcano's hotel pick-up service (www.insidethevolcano.com), which drives you by bus into the Bláfjöll mountains.

egg-yolk colour – and smell! The whole area seethes with subterranean heat, so tread carefully and stick to paths.

Just north of Krýsuvík-Seltún is ill-omened lake **Kleifarvatn** ⑮, whose waters drain and refill though no rivers run to or from it. Crime writer Arnaldur Indriðason chose the lake as the site of a gruesome corpse discovery in his murder-mystery *The Draining Lake*. Kleifarvatn is also reputed to be the home of a serpent-like monster the size of a whale.

HAFNARFJÖRÐUR

Continue on Route 42 to the old town of **Hafnarfjörður** ⑯, surrounded by Búrfell lava field and once one of Iceland's most important ports. Hafnarfjörður is well known for its 'hidden population' of supernatural creatures (from Icelandic folklore) who live in the lava. Hellisgerði Park is a *huldufólk* hotspot.

Get a sense of the town's past at **Hafnarfjörður Museum** (www.visit hafnarfjordur.is), based across four separate sites: the two main buildings are Pakkhúsið (Vesturgata 8; June–Aug daily 11am–5pm, rest of year Sat–Sun only), which contains an interesting canter through the town's history and a little toy museum; and next door Sívertsen's House (Sívertsens-Hús; June–Aug daily 11am–5pm), the 19th-century home of local bigwig, Bjarni Sívertsen.

The cool, white **Hafnarborg Centre of Culture and Fine Art** (Strandgata 34; www.hafnarborg.is; Wed–Mon noon–7pm; free), a real highlight of the town, offers art exhibitions and musical events.

Viking enthusiasts should make for Hafnarfjörður in February or June. **Fjörukráin** (Viking Village, Strandgata 50; www.fjorukrain.is) is the centre of a four-day **Viking festival** (Víkingahátíð) in mid-June, with a medieval marketplace, lamb roast, music and mock battles. During the ancient Viking month of Þorri (late Jan–late Feb), it also holds a **Þorri feast**, where you can sample the rams' testicles, cured sharkmeat and blood pudding that put the hairs on the chests of early Icelanders.

Food and drink

① KAFFI DUUS

Duusgata 10, Keflavík (Reykjanesbær); tel: 421 7080; http://duus.is; daily 11am–10pm; $$

With panoramic windows overlooking the harbour and Faxaflói Bay, Kaffi Duus is all about the sea. Duus takes greatest pride in its briny dishes: shark, cod, monkfish, langoustine or the seafood platter 'cooked with burning passion and great precision'.

② SALTHÚSIÐ

Stamphólsvegur 2, Grindavík; tel: 426 9700; www.salthusid.is; mid-May–mid-Sept daily noon–10pm, rest of year until 9pm); $$$

The town of Grindavík is the largest producer of saltfish in Iceland, so it makes sense to try some while you're here.

Reykjadalur hot river

THE SOUTHWEST

Bathe in a hot river and marvel at bleak, black beaches, before launching yourself around the 'Golden Circle' – the waterfall Gullfoss; spouting springs at Geysir; and the Unesco-listed rift valley Þingvellir. Along the coast, a world of waterfalls and frozen ice begins.

DISTANCE: 348km (216 miles)
TIME: Two days
START: Hveragerði
END: Vík
POINTS TO NOTE: If you don't have a private vehicle, seven-hour coach tours from Reykjavík cover the Golden Circle, and 10.5-hour tours cover the south coast to Vík (see Reykjavík Excursions; www.re.is). You may want to plan for activities – a bathe in the hot river above Hveragerði (bring a swimsuit), a kayak trip in Stokkseyri, snorkelling in Þingvallavatn, Super-Jeep tour to Magni and Móði craters or a glacier walk on Sólheimajökull. There are decent cafés at all three Golden Circle attractions.

The rich farming land of southwest Iceland is one of the most heavily visited regions: some of Iceland's most famous attractions are here, tied together under the label of the 'Golden Circle'. Every day coaches whizz hundreds of travellers from one natural marvel to another. But it's worth going at your own pace to appreciate Iceland's mellow rural atmosphere, investigate Saga Age ruins and wander around the enchanting natural landscapes.

HVERAGERÐI

The Ring Road east from Reykjavík brings you over the high heath and smoking earth of Hellisheiði. As the road descends, you get an aerial view of the neat streets and greenhouses of **Hveragerði** ❶ and a panorama of the southwestern plain, sea and mountains beyond. Hveragerði harnesses geothermal activity to provide the country with home-grown produce, including cut flowers and exotic bananas and papayas.

A **geothermal area**, with colourful bubbling mud and bouts of steam, appeared on the hillside above the town after a big earthquake in 2008. Lying a steep 4km (2.5-mile) walk north of town is Reykjadalur and a **hot river** ❷ where you can bathe – buy a picnic breakfast first thing from the excellent **Almar Bakeri** (see ❶) and make a morning of it.

In town, two free attractions are the

Stokkseyri Ghost Centre

cute, family-run **Hverageröi – Stone & Mineral Museum** (Ljósbrá Steinasafn; Breiðamörk 1; www.mineralsoficeland. com; Mon–Fri 9am–5pm, Sat–Sun 10am–5pm; free) at the petrol station, and **Listasafn Árnesinga** (Austurmörk 21; www.listasafnarnesinga.is; May–

Sept daily noon–6pm, Oct–Apr Thu–Sun noon–6pm), a neat modern-art gallery.

EYRARBAKKI AND STOKKSEYRI

At the main roundabout in Hverageröi, take Route 38 south (signposted to

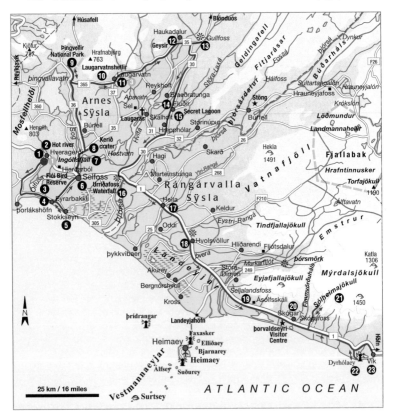

Þingvellir National Park

Eyrarbakki is famed for its seafood

Þorlákshöfn) through pancake-flat farmland, turning left onto Route 34 after about 14km (9 miles). Here the road travels over an impressive spit of land, sandwiched between the sea and Ölfusá estuary, home to **Flói Bird Reserve ❸**, a prime spot for wetland birdlife.

Eyrarbakki

Just beyond the estuary lie two tiny fishing villages that hold several visitor attractions and three highly rated seafood restaurants, including **Við Fjöruborðið** (see ❷). The more serious-minded village is **Eyrarbakki ❹**, set by the shores of a driftwood-strewn black-sand beach. This was one of Iceland's main fishing ports from the 12th to the 19th centuries, and has some picturesque restored wooden buildings. The oldest, simply called 'Húsið' ('The House'), contains the interesting little **Árnessýsla Heritage Museum** (www.husid.com; May–Sept daily 11am–6pm), with a **maritime museum** next door. As you leave Eyrarbakki heading east, Iceland's only prison, Litla Hraun, is on your right.

Stokkseyri

Five kilometres (3 miles) further along the coast road, **Stokkseyri ❺** has giddier amusements. The **Ghost Centre** at **Icelandic Wonders** (Draugasétrið; www.icelandicwonders.is; tel: 854 4510; hours vary, check website or call ahead) spooks its customers with a dark audioguided walk through Iceland's supernatural stories. It's also fun to explore the labyrinth of local waterways by kayak – **Kayakferðir** (tel: 868 9046; www.kajak.is) offers guided or do-it-yourself tours.

Make your way back to the Ring Road by following Route 34 (between Eyrarbakki and Stokkseyri) north. This takes you to **Selfoss ❻**, an unlovely but large town, full of supermarkets and other services.

THE GOLDEN CIRCLE

The Golden Circle takes in some key historical and geological attractions, including the site of the country's first parliament, an impressive geyser field and one of Iceland's most dramatic waterfalls. The whole area is rich with medieval history and saga. From Selfoss, head north on Route 35, passing **Ingólfsfjall ❼** on your left, where Ingólfur Arnarson, Iceland's First Settler, is said to be buried. At the junction with Route 36, you might want to continue on Route 35 for 5km (3 miles) to see the 55-metre (180ft)-deep **Kerið crater ❽**, blasted out 3,000 years ago and now containing a lake.

Þingvellir

Otherwise, turn north on Route 36 to reach **Þingvellir National Park ❾**, the historical heartland of Iceland, and a Unesco World Heritage Site thanks to its marvellous natural setting and unique glimpse of medieval Norse culture.

Þingvellir (parliament plains) was the site of Iceland's original Alþingi (parliament), established in 930, which laid the ground for a common culture and

Laugarvatn lake

national identity. For two weeks every summer, Icelanders flooded into the valley to trade, socialise and observe or participate in parliamentary proceedings. The last þing was held here in 1798, after which the parliament moved to Reykjavík.

There are few actual monuments or buildings to be seen, so you have to use your imagination to picture the events of the past, but the national park, a sunken rift valley between the plate boundaries, is a beautiful spot. On the horizon in every direction lie low volcanic mountains, snow-capped for much of the year. Wildflowers cover the plain in summer, and in autumn it turns sumptuous shades of red.

Above the rift, at the **Almannagjá viewing point**, a **visitor centre** (daily 9am–6.30pm, summer until 7pm) contains interactive displays about the park. From the viewing point, you can walk down a path to the Alþingi site itself: a flagpole marks the **Lögberg** ('Law Rock') from where the leader of the parliament, the law speaker, made his proclamations. Further northeast along the rift is the **Drekkingarhylur**, or 'drowning pool', where adulterous women met their ghastly fate; a little further again the pretty **Öxaráfoss waterfall** tumbles into the valley. On the eastern bank of the river is the glistening white **Þingvallabær farmhouse** and Þingvallakirkja (mid-May–Aug daily 9am–5pm).

Northeast again, near the campsite, is the main **information centre** (www. thingvellir.is; daily 9am–6pm, June–Aug until 10pm), with a café and shop selling maps and books about the area. **Dive.is** (tel: 578 6200; www.dive.is; prebooking required) offers snorkelling and scuba diving (drysuit certificate required) in the **Silfra rift**.

Laugarvatn

From Þingvellir information centre, head south along Route 36 before turning left onto Route 365 to Laugarvatn. After 10km (6 miles), make a quick 3km (2 mile) side stop on Route 367 to see **Laugarvatnshellir ⑩** (July–Aug daily 10am–6pm), a cave used over the centuries as a sheep shelter and in the 1920s as a home. Reconstructed in 2017, the house is now a cute hobbit-like structure with a lava ceiling and walls – the café here also serves good coffee and waffles.

Laugarvatn ⑪, on the shore of a lake of the same name, is another small town built on a geothermal spring. You can bathe in the mineral-rich waters at **Laugarvatn Fontana Geothermal Baths** (tel: 486 1400; www.fontana.is; daily early June–Aug 10am–11pm, rest of the year 11am–10pm), which has warm pools, hot pots and three steam rooms. Their café also sells lava bread baked in the hot black sand.

Two hundred metres/yds away, the historical hot spring **Vígðalaug** was used as an all-weather baptism spot by Iceland's first Christians.

The town is a popular holiday spot for Icelanders, and is a good place to

Strokkur geyser erupts every 10 minutes to please the crowds

break up your trip. There are two Edda hotels, good food at **Lindin** (see ③) and lots of activities including sailing, fishing, golf, Super Jeep tours and caving (with **Laugarvatn Adventure** – tel: 888 1922; www.caving.is).

Geysir

Take Route 37 northeast out of Laugarvatn. After 20km (12 miles), turn left onto Route 35 – the next Golden Circle target is just 5km (3 miles) away at **Geysir** ⑫, which gave its name to all such water spouts around the world. Sadly, the **Great Geysir**, which started erupting in the 13th century and once reached heights of up to 80 metres (260ft), has been dormant for decades. An earthquake in 2000 briefly woke it up: it erupted for two days straight, reaching 122 metres (400ft) in height, then settled into slumber once again.

Luckily, the Great Geysir's ever-reliable neighbour, **Strokkur** ('the churn'), bursts upwards every 10 minutes or so to a height of up to 30 metres (100ft). Stand up-wind of its bulging blue eye to avoid the scalding water.

The whole area is geothermically active, with walking trails marked out among steaming vents, turquoise pools and glistening, multicoloured mud formations.

Gullfoss

From Geysir, drive another 9km (6 miles) along Route 35 for the third Golden Circle treat. **Gullfoss** ⑬ (Golden Falls; http://gullfoss.is) is a deafening double water-fall, where the River Hvítá drops 32 metres (105ft) before thundering away down a 2km (1.2-mile)-long canyon. A path from the parking area leads down to the waterfall's northern face, allowing you to feel the thunder at close range. Wear something waterproof, or the clouds of spray that create photogenic rainbows on sunny days will douse you from head to foot.

By the café, a small exhibition space remembers Sigríður Tómasdóttir, a local farmer's daughter who in the 1920s protested against plans to build a dam above Gullfoss. The government ended up purchasing the falls and making them a national monument.

Flúðir

From Gullfoss, head south on Route 30, through **Flúðir** ⑭, another very active geothermal area, famous for its mushroom-growing. Shortly after passing the campsite, and just before crossing a little stream, take the small road on your left signposted to Hvammur to reach the **Secret Lagoon** ⑮ (tel: 555 3351; www.secretlagoon.is; daily May–Sept 10am–10pm, Oct–Apr 11am–8pm – ticket sales stop 50 minutes before closing), a lovely natural geothermal pool with bubbling hot springs nearby.

THE RING ROAD TO VÍK

Hella and Hvolsvöllur

Return to Route 30, which ends back at the Ring Road. As you turn east onto Route 1, the first river you cross is the

Vík town with Reynisdrangar in the distance

Þjórsá ⑯, Iceland's longest. Here you'll find the low but powerful **Urriðafoss** falls, full of leaping salmon and sea trout during breeding season.

The unassuming towns of **Hella** ⑰ and **Hvolsvöllur** ⑱, with around 800 and 900 inhabitants respectively, are the biggest settlements for the next 360km (225 miles). Looming ominously beyond the flat farmland is the snow-capped volcano **Hekla** often wreathed in clouds. In medieval times, the volcano had a fearsome reputation – it was believed to be a gateway to hell. Hekla is very active, with eruptions in 1970, 1980, 1991 and 2000.

This area is also the setting for one of the best-loved Icelandic sagas, *Njáls Saga*. The **Saga Centre** (www.njala.is; mid-May–mid-Sept daily 9am–6pm, mid-Sept–mid-May Sat–Sun 10am–5pm) in Hvolsvöllur, signposted from the main road, has a simple exhibition telling the story.

> ## Þórsmörk
>
> Literally 'Thor's forest', Þórsmörk is one of Iceland's most spectacular but inaccessible wilderness areas. It is sealed off by three glaciers, two deep rivers and a string of mountains, and the single dirt road is only passable to 4WDs. You will have to make a separate trip here – the scheduled bus 9/9a runs daily May to September, collecting passengers at Seljalandsfoss, among other places (see www.re.is for details).

Opened in 2017 and also in Hvolsvöllur, the **Lava Centre** (tel: 415 5200; http://lavacentre.is; daily 9am–7pm) is an interactive, high-tech exhibition examining Iceland's volcanoes, lava flows, eruptions, earthquakes and glacial floods. A map in the entrance shows seismic activity across Iceland over the previous 48 hours, and earthquake simulations, recreated magma chambers and a volcano film leave you in no doubt about the drama that such activity can unleash.

Skógar

Twenty kilometres (12 miles) east of Hvolsvöllur is the turnoff to **Landeyjahöfn** (Route 251), from where the ferry to the Vestmannaeyjar (see page 56) departs. Continuing a short distance along the Ring Road, cross the sparkling water and black sand of the Markarfljót river and look out for the silvery stream of **Seljalandsfoss** ⑲ waterfall. Next to the waterfall is the turnoff to Route F249, which leads to **Þórsmörk** (see box).

Ten kilometres (6 miles) east of Seljalandsfoss is the tiny village of **Skógar** ⑳, home to a fantastic **folk museum** (www.skogasafn.is; daily June–Aug 9am–6pm, Sept–May 10am–5pm). It contains a 15,000-piece collection, including a reconstructed church, a school and a driftwood house. Another stunner of a waterfall crashes down from nearby cliffs – 62-metre (203ft) -high **Skógafoss** is extraordinarily photogenic. Look out for glints of gold

Thundering Seljalandsfoss waterfall

within – legend tells that the first settler at Skógar hid his treasure beneath the falls.

This area sits under **Eyjafjallajökull** famous for the subglacial volcano that erupted in 2010, covering everything for miles around in thick grey ash and resulting in the largest air-traffic shutdown since World War II. Volcano enthusiasts may want to stay overnight in Skógar and join a five-hour Super Jeep tour and hike (guidetoiceland.is) to see the steaming craters Magni and Móði, created during the eruption.

Vík and around

Five kilometres (3 miles) east of Skógar, Route 221 takes a twisting, turning, near-vertical ascent up to **Sólheima-jökull ㉑**, where the Icelandic Mountain Guides (www.mountainguides.is) offer daily glacier walks exploring a world of water cauldrons, crevasses and ancient ash – book ahead.

Turn off onto Route 218, 12km (7 miles) further down the Ring Road, to reach the distinctive rock arch at **Dyrhólaey ㉒**, a nature reserve packed full of nesting seabirds, and **Reynisfjara** beach, with black sand and basalt columns. Keep well away from the water – freak waves have killed several people over the years.

The last major stop is the coastal town of **Vík ㉓**, set beside a dramatic stretch of coastline: here the North Atlantic swell smashes down onto a long beach of black sand and three distinctive stone steeples, known as **Reynisdrangar**, rise out of the sea. Legend has it that they are trolls who were turned to stone as they pulled their three-masted ship ashore. Far more monstrous are the aggressive Arctic terns – Vík contains one of Iceland's largest breeding colonies.

Food and drink

❶ ALMAR BAKERI
Sunnumörk 2, Hveragerði; tel: 483 1919;
Mon–Sat 7am–6pm, Sun 8am–6pm; $
Delectable pastries, cakes, sandwiches and coffee, served with a smile.

❷ VIÐ FJÖRUBORÐIÐ
Eyrarbraut 3, Stokkseyri; tel: 483 1550;
www.fjorubordid.is; daily noon–9pm; $$$
A renowned lobster (really langoustine) restaurant by the sea. The short menu features little more than lobster soup and lobster tails in garlic, but these are so good that Reykjavík's citizens drive the 120km (75-mile) round trip just to enjoy them.

❸ LINDIN RESTAURANT
Lindarbraut 2, Laugarvatn; tel: 486 1262;
www.laugarvatn.is; daily noon–9pm; $$$
Wild game and fresh trout, caught daily from the lake on the restaurant's doorstep, are served in both the bistro and the fine-dining restaurant. Chef Baldur modestly touts his chocolate mousse as 'the best in the world'!

Heimaey harbour

HEIMAEY

The Vestmannaeyjar – 16 tiny islands – rise rugged and inhospitable from the cold sea, combining seductive isolation with raw natural beauty. The largest of the archipelago is friendly Heimaey, with a fascinating history, explored in interesting museums, and blustery clifftop walks that will blow your socks off.

DISTANCE: Heimaey town walk: 7km (4 miles); Storhöfði walk: 12km (7.5 miles)
TIME: Two days
START: Heimaey harbour
END: Heimaey swimming pool
POINTS TO NOTE: You could take your car on the ferry, but Heimaey is very walkable and this two-day route is all on foot. For the Heimaey town walk, book on the 4pm boat tour (Viking Tours; tel: 488 4884; www.vikingtours.is) of the island. If you don't want to walk to Storhöfði, consider an island bus tour (Viking Tours, as above) or horse-riding tour (Lyngfell Stables; tel: 898 1809; www.facebook.com/Lyngfell) instead.

The only inhabited island in the Vestmannaeyjar archipelago is **Heimaey**, which can be reached by plane from Reykjavík or by ferry from Landeyjarhöfn (or Þorlákshöfn under certain tide/weather conditions). This route includes a 7km (4-mile) walk around town and a 12km (7.5-mile) round trip to **Storhöfði**.

In contrast to its harsh surroundings, Heimaey is one of the friendliest places in Iceland, its sense of community forged by isolation and fickle nature. The town's precarious position on top of a volcano was brought into sharp focus on 23 January 1973, when a mile-long fissure cracked open without warning, and a wall of molten lava poured towards the town. By great good fortune, the entire fishing fleet was docked that night: the island was evacuated, with not one life lost. Over the next five months, 33 million tonnes of lava spewed from the fissure, burying houses and devastating the island. The eruption was over by July, and residents started returning to their altered home: the island was 2.2 sq km (0.84 sq miles) larger, and boasted a new mountain, Eldfell.

HEIMAEY TOWN CENTRE

Harbour to Skansinn

Heimaey town ❶ depends upon its **harbour Ⓐ**, home to its fleet of colourful fishing trawlers, the life's blood of

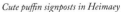

Stafkirkjan   *Cute puffin signposts in Heimaey*

the local community. The 1973 eruption almost eradicated it, when a 165-metre (500ft) wall of molten lava threatened to block the harbour entrance. Two commercial dredging ships pumped 43 million litres (11.5 million gallons) of water a day over the lava to cool it, miraculously stopping the flow and averting disaster. In fact, residents say that the lava improved the harbour, creating a natural windbreak better to shelter the fleet.

The harbour is also where the ferry *Herjólfur* disgorges its passengers from the mainland. Walk up Skildingavegur, then turn left onto Strandvegur, passing the **tourist information office 🅑**, to reach one of Heimaey's most picturesque areas, **Skansinn 🅒**. A 15th-century fortress once defended the harbour – although to no avail when trouble came. In 1627 Algerian pirates skirted the defences and landed on the south side of the island, capturing 242 islanders to sell as slaves. Little remains of the fort, but the view is pretty, looking down onto **Landlyst**, once the island's maternity hospital, and **Stafkirkjan**, a stave church presented to Heimaey in 2000 by the Norwegian government to celebrate 1,000 years of Christianity. Behind you is the northwestern edge of the lava flow that extended the island in 1973.

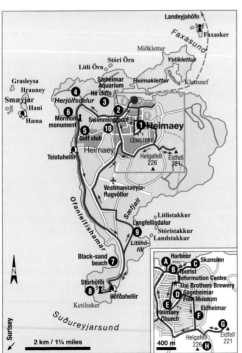

Folk museum and church

Retrace your steps, turning left up Barustígur to pick up a picnic lunch at **Stofan Bakhús** (see **1**). Cross the central park/plaza, arriving at the town's **Sagnheimar**

Helgafell volcano

Folk Museum (www.sagnheimar.is; May–Sept daily 10am–5pm, Oct–Apr Mon–Sat 1–4pm) above the library, for opening time. The museum has been revamped, with permanent exhibitions on the pirate raids; harrowing tales of a fisherman's life at sea; the Þjóðhátíð Festival, first held in 1874; and the 1973 eruption and evacuation.

Turn left out of the museum, then left again up Skólavegur to the picturesque white **church** , with a statue commemorating the island's fishermen lost at sea. Across the road, the **cemetery** was completely buried by ash in 1973, with just the arch of the gateway standing out.

Volcano museum and volcano

To find out more about the volcanic devastation, head down Kirkjuvegur, turn right onto Birkihlíð, then right up Helgafellsbraut. Here, a multimedia museum, **Eldheimar** (http://eldheimar.is; May–Sept daily 11am–6pm, Oct–Apr Wed–Sun 1–5pm), has been built around a house excavated from the lava flow – one of 370 homes that were buried. An excellent audioguide gives first-hand accounts of the drama.

Now it's time to visit the cause of all the trouble. Head to the top of Helgafellsbraut, turning left onto Fellavegur, then left onto a rough and cindery walking path to the top of **Eldfell** , the 221-metre (725ft)-high peak formed during the eruption. The spectacular view from the top clearly shows how a full one-sixth of the island was created by the fresh lava flow. The vista stretches across brightly painted corrugated iron roofs to the harbour and, on a clear day, to the mainland. Crack out the picnic lunch while enjoying the stunning views. While you're eating, dig a few inches down into the ground to feel the still-present volcanic heat.

Come back down the volcano, walking along Fellavegur, which skirts the edge of an older cone **Helgafell** , to Strembugata. Heading straight down this street will lead you, via several name changes, back to the harbour for a 4pm boat tour.

Sailing round the island

A visit to Heimaey would not be complete without an excursion on the waves. **Viking Tours** (tel: 488 4884; www.vikingtours.is; mid-May–mid-Sept daily 11am and 4pm) sails a small boat from the harbour, bouncing around the whole island and finishing with a saxophone solo inside the echoing **Klettshellur** sea cave. The 1.5-hour trip gives views of Heimaey's steep cliffs crowded with seabirds; if you're lucky, you might also see whales out to sea. You also get good views of the other jagged outcrops in the island chain, visited in spring by islanders who collect birds' eggs and hunt puffins there. To the southwest, **Surtsey** emerged from the sea in an underwater eruption in the mid-1960s. It is off limits to tourists: only a few scientists are given permis-

Photogenic Atlantic puffins

sion to visit, as the island is providing unique and invaluable data on how virgin habitats are colonised by plant and animal life.

Back on dry land, there are several good restaurants, such as **Slippurinn** (see ❷), for an evening meal near the harbour. Hótel Vestmannaeyjar is a good place to overnight (see page 115).

A WALK TO STORHÖFÐI

Heimaey's coves, inlets and towering cliffs, often battered by rain and wind, make for bracing walks. One such is along the west coast to Storhöfði.

Pop into the bakery again to pick up a picnic lunch. To put you in a nature-y mood, start the walk with a visit to **Sæheimar Aquarium** ❷ (http://sae heimar.is; May–Sept daily 10am–5pm, Oct–Apr Mon–Fri 2–3.30pm, Sat 1–4pm), where there is a small display of live Icelandic fish, mostly brought in by fishermen. The aquarium also acts as a bird rescue centre and sometimes has puffin chicks in season – they may absolutely reek of fish, but still it's delightful to get so close to a puffling.

Há cliffs and Herjólfsdalur

From the aquarium, head downhill, turning left onto Vesturvegur, left again onto Flatir, then follow Hlíðarvegur left around the **Há cliffs** ❸. Here you might see people practising the island's 'sport' *sprang*, the daredevil technique

of rappelling from the cliffs, traditionally in order to collect birds' eggs.

After half a kilometre, the road leads to **Herjólfsdalur** ❹. This luscious green crater was once thought to be the home of the island's first settler, Herjólfur Barðursson, but archaeologists recently unearthed the foundations of Herjólfur's house next to the **golf club** ❺.

The puffin population

The colourful Atlantic puffin – with its large, stripy beak and bright orange legs and feet – is a great favourite with visitors. Puffins are highly sociable, often standing about in groups and nesting in large colonies. They fish together, too, forming wide rafts out to sea, diving to depths of 60 metres (200ft) in search of their main food, sand eels.

Both parents share child-rearing responsibilities. They dig burrows deep into the cliff sides, and stand guard over their precious single egg, rarely travelling far from the colony while raising their young.

Traditionally, puffins are hunted for food in Iceland, fished out of the air with huge nets. They produce a dark meat, like duck but less fatty, often served with a blueberry sauce. However, concerns over declining colonies have led to a hunting ban in the Vestmannaeyjar, once the capital of puffins and puffin-hunting.

Eastern cliffs

Near the beginning of the cliff-top path is a **monument** ❻ to 200 Heimaey inhabitants who converted to Mormonism and emigrated to Utah between 1854 and 1914. The path continues past the golf course, over crumbling cliffs full of mixed **seabird colonies**, including gannets, shearwaters, storm petrels and guillemots. Millions of puffins used to come here to breed in cliff-top burrows, although numbers have declined rapidly in recent years.

Passing curiosities such as a tractor stuck halfway down a cliff, a shipwreck memorial and fish-drying racks, you reach a narrow isthmus with a **black-sand beach** ❼. On the other side of the road is another black-sand bay, **Ræningjatangi**, where pirates landed during the 1627 raid.

Storhöfði

The isthmus joins the main bulk of the island to **Storhöfði** ❽. Find a sheltered spot to eat your picnic lunch before rounding the island's southernmost tip, which is the windiest place in Iceland – gales of 250kph (150mph) and waves of 23 metres (75ft) have been recorded here during storms. Here you'll find a **bird hide** where you can watch puffins, as well as the oldest **lighthouse** in Iceland.

Back to town

Back past the isthmus on the eastern shore is **Lyngfellisdalur** ❾, with fabulous views that take in all of the Vestmannaeyjar islands. The airport runway prevents you continuing along the east coast, so follow the road back to town. Call for an evening dip at the town's good **swimming pool** ❿ (June–Aug Mon–Fri 6.15am–9pm, Sat–Sun 9am–6pm, Sept–May Mon–Fri 2–9pm, Sat–Sun 9am–5pm), with slides, sauna and three hot tubs. Alternatively, say to heck with it and end your blustery walk with a beer at the excellent microbrewery, **The Brothers Brewery** (http://tbb.is; Thu 4pm–11pm, Fri–Sat 2pm–1am), opened in 2016.

Food and drink

❶ STOFAN BAKHÚS

Barustígur 7; tel: 481 2424; www.face book.com/stofanbakhus; Mon–Fri 8am–5pm, Sat–Sun 9am–5pm; $
Great selection of sumptuous baked goods and fine coffee.

❷ SLIPPURINN

Strandvegur 76; tel: 481 1515; http://slippurinn.com; May–Sept 5–10pm; $$$$
In a former workshop by the harbour, this family-run restaurant specialises in fish and shellfish. Five set menus show off signature dishes, such as langoustine soup or marinated scallops with rhubarb and angelica. Vegetarians get a whole menu of their own.

Biking around Skaftafell

THE SOUTHEAST

The enormous Vatnajökull ice cap overshadows the region, sending its glaciers flowing down the mountains into a beautiful wasteland of sand and water. The highlight is the rugged and popular Skaftafell area of Vatnajökull National Park.

DISTANCE: 200km (125 miles)
TIME: A full day
START: Kirkjubæjarklaustur
END: Höfn
POINTS TO NOTE: Southeast Iceland is a wilderness, with few eating and accommodation options – the latter should be booked in advance. You might want to build in an extra day to take a mountain-bus tour to Laki (see page 63 and Reykjavík Excursions' website, www.re.is, for details).

The Vatnajökull icecap, and its seven subterranean volcanoes, dominates southeastern Iceland. When the volcanoes erupt, the ice melts and explosive torrents of floodwater and debris (known as *jökulhlaups*), as large in volume as the Amazon River, surge down to the sea. Much of the landscape is made up of *sandur*, great plains of silt, sand and gravel, dotted with boulders, which have all been dumped by the floods. Vatnajökull's glacial flows made much of the coast almost impassable

for centuries: the Ring Road was only completed in 1974.

Huge swathes of this brutally beautiful landscape were also shaped by the eruption of the Lakagígar craters in 1783 – known as the Laki eruptions, after a nearby mountain, this was one of the worst natural disasters in recorded history.

KIRKJUBÆJARKLAUSTUR

In the middle of the wasteland is the tiny hamlet of **Kirkjubæjarklaustur ❶** – often shortened to 'Klaustur' – perhaps protected from biblical-scale fire and floods by its long association with godly folk. Kirkjubæjarklaustur was first settled by Irish monks, who were driven out by the Vikings but left a curse that no pagan would ever live here. In 1186, Benedictine nuns set up a convent, although it wasn't exactly a model institution – two nuns were burned at the stake, one for blaspheming against the Pope, the other for sleeping with the devil. Named after the nuns, waterfall **Systrafoss** sprays down from steep cliffs behind the ham-

let, running from the lake **Systravatn** where the Benedictine sisters bathed.

During the 1783 Laki eruptions, the local pastor delivered the ultimate fire-and-brimstone sermon to his flock, as chunks of ash pelted from the sky and a flow of lava headed inexorably towards the hamlet. When the sermon ended, the congregation stumbled outside to find that the lava had miraculously changed course, sparing the church and people. **Steingrímsson memorial chapel**, built in 1974 on the site of the old church, commemorates this neat piece of divine intervention.

Just over the field from the campsite is the curious **Kirkjugólf** – the name means 'church floor' – a small, natural formation of hexagonal basalt columns.

Skaftárstofa tourist information office (www.visitklaustur.is; early Apr–Aug daily 9am–6pm) is located on the left as you drive through the village, and has exhibitions and films about Vatnajökull and the Laki eruption; **Systrakaffi**, see ①, makes a good food stop.

EAST THROUGH SKEIÐARÁRSANDUR

The Ring Road east from Kirkjubæjarklaustur runs past attractive **Foss á Síðu** ② farm, 10km (6 miles) away, named for the thin waterfall above it. On the other

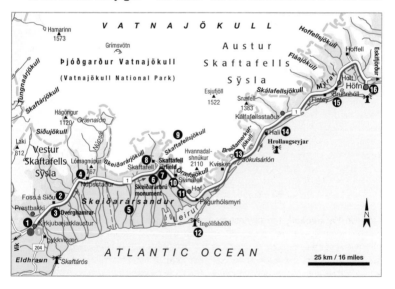

Exploring the lava field at Laki

side of the road, 700 metres (765yds) away, are the **Dverghamrar** ❸ (Dwarf Rocks) basalt columns. Cross a sunken plain of moss-covered lava – created by the Laki eruptions – to the farm of **Núpsstaður** ❹, where you'll find one of Iceland's most charming 17th-century buildings, a turf church with a working antique harmonium.

At this point begins **Skeiðarársandur** ❺, the biggest of the southern *sandurs* – great wastelands of black sand and glacial debris carried out by volcanic eruptions from underneath Vatnajökull. In November 1996, a glacial burst from the Grímsvötn caldera covered Skeiðarársandur in black and muddy floodwater, ripping up electric cables, and sweeping away two bridges and a 12km (7-mile) stretch of the Ring Road. The **Skeiðarárbrú monument** ❻ displays two steel bridge girders, pounded to junk by ice blocks weighing hundreds of tons.

Treacherous to some, this inhospitable wasteland is a cosy creche to others – Skeiðarársandur is one of the most important breeding areas for great skuas in the northern hemisphere.

VATNAJÖKULL NATIONAL PARK

Massive **Vatnajökull**, the biggest icecap outside the poles, is almost 150km (90 miles) across and dominates the southeastern corner of Iceland. Its size and beauty is best appreciated from the air: you can take a 45-minute sightseeing flight from **Skaftafell airfield** ❼ (tel: 854 4105; www.flightseeing.is).

In June 2008, Vatnajökull National Park was created to protect the icecap.

Bus trip to Laki

Many people stay in Kirkjubæjarklaustur as a jumping-off point to the infamous Lakagígar crater row, only accessible by 4WD vehicle in summer. During the 1783 eruptions, 30 billion tonnes of lava poured from the craters over the course of 10 months – one of the largest effusive eruptions ever recorded. Houses and farms were obliterated, and clouds of sulphur dioxide and fluorine killed plants and lifestock, causing the 'Haze Famine' that killed a quarter of the population.

Today this unearthly and surprisingly fragile environment nestles within the protective boundaries of Vatnajökull National Park. There are fantastic views to be had from the top of Mt Laki: around 120 craters extend for 25km (15 miles) up to the glacier, and the surrounding lava field is dotted with caves and other lava formations. Scheduled bus service 16 runs daily mid-June to August, collecting passengers from Skaftafell service centre at 8am and the N1 petrol station in Kirkjubæjarklaustur at 9am; visitors have around four hours to explore the craters, returning to Kirkjubæjarklaustur at 8pm and Skaftafell at 9pm. Take refreshments with you.

Immense Skaftafellsjökull glacier

At a mighty 13,600 sq km (5,300 sq miles), covering 13 percent of Iceland's total area, Vatnajökull is now Europe's largest national park. **Skaftafell** ❽ is the most popular area of the park, with two Saga Age farms, rugged mountains, waterfalls and three glaciers that flow down from the icecap.

The park service operates an **Information Centre** (tel: 470 8300; www.vatnajokulsthjodgardur.is; daily May–Sept 9am–7pm, Oct–Nov 9am–6pm, Dec–Feb 9am–5pm, Mar–Apr 9am–6pm) and café next to a parking area and a large, raucous camping ground.

Shorter walks in the park include the route up to **Svartifoss** (Black Falls), named after the surrounding cliffs of sombre black basalt, and the wheelchair-accessible path to the edge of the **Skaftafellsjökull** ❾ glacier tongue. If you want to get up onto the glaciers, several companies (Icelandic Mountain Guides: www.mountainguides.is; Glacier Guides: http://glacierguides.is) have summer huts in the parking area, offering guided walks with crampons and ice axes. If you have time to explore the park in more depth, there are several daylong and overnight routes to the higher moorlands and peaks – ask for details at the information centre.

As you leave Skaftafell on the Ring Road east, you pass the farm **Svínafell** ❿, the home of Flosi Þórðarson, who murdered Njáll and his family in *Njáls Saga*. A further 11km (7 miles) along is the farm **Hof** ⓫, which offers picturesque accommodation and has the last turf church to be built in Iceland. Both farms sit under the shadow of the glacier **Öræfajökull**, whose peak, **Hvannadalshnúkur**, is the highest in Iceland at 2,120 metres/6,950ft.

INGÓLFSHÖFÐI

Just south of Hof, the promontory **Ingólfshöfði** ⓬ is where the First Settler, Ingólfur Arnarson, spent his first winter in Iceland. The headland is now a **nature reserve**, perfect for birdwatchers, and accessed by **guided haycart tour** (www.fromcoasttomountains.com; May–Aug Mon–Sat 1.15pm) across the black-sand estuary, departing from Ingólfshöfði car parking (the turn-off is signposted between the farms Hofsnes and Fagurhólsmýri). Birdwatching is at its best during the breeding season in May and June.

JÖKULSÁRLÓN

Continuing east, the next major point of interest is the extraordinary glacier river lagoon at **Jökulsárlón** ⓭. Great slabs of ice that have broken off **Breiðamerkurjökull** glacier float serenely in the water, some as big as houses. The lake only formed in the 20th century, but climate change has seen the glacier melt so quickly that Jökulsárlón is now the deepest lake in Iceland. **Boat trips** (http://icelagoon.is; 40 per day July–Aug, fewer at other times) weave among

Jökulsárlón glacial lagoon

the glistening ice formations, although you can see the icebergs just as well from the shoreline. James Bond fans may get a sense of déjà vu here – the opening scenes of the film *A View to a Kill* were shot here, as well as part of *Die Another Day*.

HÖFN AND AROUND

Twelve kilometres (7 miles) past Jökulsárlón, local guides from **Hali** ⓮ can take you on **glacier walks** or to visit **ice caves** – see www.glacier adventure.is for details. Also at Hali is **Þórbergssetur** (www.thorbergur. is; daily 9am–8pm), a museum in memory of author Þórbergur Þórðarson (1888–1974) who lived at the farm. Unfortunately, almost none of his ground-breaking, satirical work has been translated into English, but the museum is nevertheless an interesting look at rural life in 19th- and 20th-century Iceland.

The river valleys along this stretch of the Ring Road are beautiful but thinly populated, inhabited mainly by birds, and a herd of cows at **Brunnhóll** ⓯ (http://brunnholl.is) who provide the milk for Jöklaís ice cream, made on the farm – pop in to try some.

Eventually, you'll come to the town of **Höfn** ⓰ ('harbour'), the largest settlement for miles around, in a beautiful setting on **Hornafjörður** fjord. Höfn is famous for its langoustines, and is liveliest during the annual **Lobster Festi-**

val (Humarhátíð; www.facebook.com/ Humarhatid) held at the end of June. There is a **National Park Visitor Centre** (Gamlabúð; tel: 470 8330; www.vatnajokulsthjodgardur.is; daily June–Aug 9am–7pm, May and Sept 9am–6pm, rest of the year 9am–5pm), set in an elegantly restored 150-year-old wooden building by the harbour. An exhibition explains the region's geology, glaciers, natural history and culture. Tours of Vatnajökull ice cap by 4WD can be organised from Höfn.

South of the harbour is **Ósland**, a promontory with rich birdlife (particularly Arctic tern), from where there are fabulous mountain-and-glacier views.

East of Höfn along the Ring Road, you will pass nothing but stark mountains, silent lagoons and rocky bays, isolated farmhouses and the odd lonely lighthouse until you reach the next sprawling metropolis, Djúpivogur (see page 66).

Food and drink

① SYSTRAKAFFI

Klausturvegur 13, Kirkjubæjarklaustur; tel: 487 4848; www.systrakaffi.is; daily noon–9pm; $$

Surrounded by glacial wastelands, this village of 140 souls feels like a metropolis, with Systrakaffi its warm, buzzing soul. Thaw out with a large latte, tasty homemade cakes, deep bowls of fresh soup and slabs of crispy Arctic char.

Hallormsstaðaskógur 'forest'

THE EAST FJORDS

Most visitors zip through the east en route to elsewhere, missing the appeal of its sparkling fjords and peaceful fishing villages. Wildlife is all around, from herds of reindeer to the (mythical?) monster that dwells in lake Lögurinn...

DISTANCE: 240km (150 miles)
TIME: Two days
START: Djúpivogur
END: Egilsstaðir
POINTS TO NOTE: Egilsstaðir breaks up the two legs of this route, and is the natural place to overnight (see Accommodation, page 112). There are two additional side trips (see boxes pages 68 and 69) that also start in Egilsstaðir – depending on your interests and available time.

The eastern fjords are less dramatic than those in the west, but are still charming. Little fishing villages get on with life, with a few concessions to tourists in the form of some interesting museums.

Near Egilsstaðir, Lögurinn lake, bordered by the country's largest forest, is a popular holiday spot for Icelanders. Westward, in the dry interior, starkly beautiful wilderness areas are populated by pink-footed geese and herds of roaming reindeer.

FOLLOWING THE FJORDS

Djúpivogur ❶ is the first fishing village east of Höfn, a sprawling metropolis of 349 people. The oldest building, dating back to 1790, holds the cultural centre, **Langabúð** (tel: 478 8220; 15 May–15 Sept, call for hours), with an exhibition about Icelandic sculptor Ríkarður Jónsson, who was born in the village; a heritage collection in the loft; and a pleasant **café**, see ❶. Puffin fans might want to stick around until 1pm, when a four-hour **guided tour** (tel: 478 8119; www.djupivogur.is/papey; June–Aug daily) heads from the jetty below Langabúð to the uninhabited island of **Papey** ❷, home to 30,000 puffin pairs.

Follow Route 1 around Berufjörður, past Berunes youth hostel and **Havari farm** ❸ (www.havari.is), which holds some amazing Saturday-night gigs in summer, and over an impressive 2km (1.2 mile) causeway. Here, Route 1 turns abruptly northwards at Breiðdalsvík. If you're in a hurry, you can follow it to Egilsstaðir (see page 68). Otherwise, continue up and down the fjord-lined coast on Route 96, a

Djúpivogur   *Petra's Stone and Mineral Collection*

slower but better-paved and more scenic route, with small villages squeezed between the choppy North Atlantic and steep mountains.

Make a stop in **Stöðvarfjörður ❹** to visit **Petra's Stone and Mineral Collection** (www.steinapetra.is; May–mid-Oct daily 9am–6pm, mid-Oct–Nov and Feb–Apr Mon–Fri 9am–3pm), amassed by Petra Sveinsdóttir over a long lifetime, in a bungalow on the main road.

Thirty kilometres (19 miles) along the weaving coastline, **Fáskrúðsfjörður ❺** has an interesting history. In the late

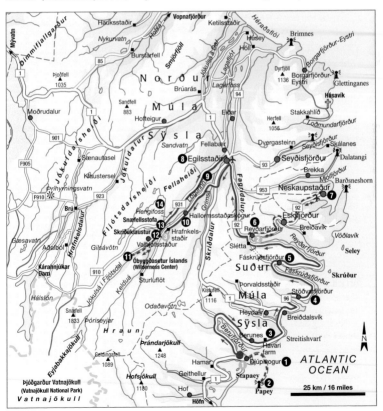

Colourful roofs and kayaks at Seyðisfjörður

19th century, this village was home to French sailors, who had their own hospital, church and graveyard. **Fransmenn á Íslandi** (tel: 475 1170; mid-May–mid-Sept daily 10am–6pm) recreates their living conditions.

Seyðisfjörður side trip

From Egilsstaðir, Route 93 runs due east over Mt Bjólfur, with spectacular views over the sparkling water and pretty fishing village of Seyðisfjörður, worth a half-day side trip for the scenic drive alone. The village's colourful wooden houses, shipped over in kit form from Norway in the 1930s, are the first thing that passengers arriving in Iceland on the Smyril Line ferry see. Seyðisfjörður springs to life when the ship docks, on Thursdays in high summer and Tuesdays in the shoulder season.

Seyðisfjörður has a healthy cultural life: the picturesque Bláa kirkjan (Blue Church) organises classical, jazz, blues and folk concerts on Wednesday evenings in July and early August; Skaftfell Center for Visual Art (http://skaftfell.is) stages contemporary art exhibitions and has a good bistro where you can stop for coffee or lunch if you need to refuel; and the unusual sound-sculpture Tvísöngur, inspired by ancient two-part singing, is a worthwhile 20-minute walk up the mountainside.

The tranquil fjord makes a great place for guided kayak tours (Hlynur Oddsson; tel: 865 3741).

The next fjord along is the longest and widest in the east, and was once filled with Norwegian whaling stations; today, the huge aluminium smelter at **Reyðarfjörður** ⑥ is the biggest employer. Make for **Tærgesen** ② to refill the tank, before heading to the town's fascinating little museum, the **Icelandic Wartime Museum** (Stríðsárasafnið; Austurvegur; June–Aug daily 1–5pm), which focuses on the billeting of 3,000 Allied soldiers here during World War II, and the impact that had on local people.

Route 92 then continues east through **Eskifjörður** to **Neskaupstaður** ⑦, where the road ends. If you have time for the 80km/50-mile return-trip, it's worth it for the sheer end-of-the-world feel. Alternatively, head straight for Egilsstaðir.

EGILSSTAÐIR

From Reyðarfjörður, head west then north on Route 92 to the region's most important crossroad, **Egilsstaðir** ⑧ (population 2,400). The town had a growth spurt in the 2000s when it serviced construction workers on Kárahnjúkar dam and Reyðarfjörður aluminium smelter, and is something of an urban sprawl, but it makes a convenient place to stop overnight (for accommodation options, see page 116).

LAKE LÖGURINN

South of Egilsstaðir stretches the long, thin, milky-coloured lake **Lögurinn** ⑨,

Borgarfjörður Eystri campsite

created by the glacial Lagarfljót river. Over 100 metres (330ft) deep, the lake is said to be home to a monster – sightings of Lagarfljótsormur have been recorded from the 14th century up to the present day.

Eastern shore

Head south out of town on Route 1, turning right at the junction with Route 931 and following the road along the eastern shore to **Hallormsstaðaskógur** ⑩. Iceland's largest 'forest' is revered by Icelanders, for whom trees are a rarity. Hallormsstaðaskógur began as a reforestation experiment, and was so successful that its arboretum now contains 70 tree species. Well-marked trails run through the woods for a pleasant 30-minute stroll.

South of the lake

Turn left onto Route 933, which crosses the far end of the lake. For a wild detour, turn left again onto Route 9340 and continue for 9km (5.5 miles), until you reach the **Wilderness Center** ⑪ (Óbyggðasetur Íslands; www.wilderness.is; mid-May–Sept daily 8am–10pm), a jack-of-all-trades place with accommodation, food, a carefully curated exhibition on rural life and hikes and horse rides in the lovely waterfall-filled valleys around the old farm.

Western shore

Otherwise, turn right up the west shore of lake Lögurinn. Just up the road is

Borgarfjörður Eystri side trip

Another spectacular excursion from Egilsstaðir is to Borgarfjörður Eystri, also known as Bakkagerði, reached by following Route 94 north for 70km (43 miles). The highway passes through marshland crowded with birdlife, before rising over a high pass, where Dyrfjöll ('Gate Mountains'), a distinctive mountain range with a great 'doorway' cutting through it, comes into view. In medieval times, a monstrous creature named Naddi used to crawl out of the sea here and attack late-night travellers, before he was vanquished by a brave local.

These dramatic mountains are rich in semi-precious stones like rhyolite, jasper and agate, which are polished into shiny trinkets for sale at Álfacafé. The renowned landscape artist Jóhannes Kjarval was born in Borgarfjörður. He painted the altarpiece in the town's church, which depicts a very Icelandic 'Sermon on the Mount', with Jesus preaching in front of Dyrfjöll mountains. Across the street is the colourful turf house Lindarbakki, a private residence, and towards the beach a stone hillock called Álfaborg ('elf hill'), where the queen of Iceland's hidden people is said to live. At Hafnarhólmi, the small boat harbour, there is an excellent bird-watching hide perfect for puffin-spotting.

Skriðuklaustur ⑫ (www.skriduklaus
tur.is; daily June–Aug 10am–6pm,
May and Sept noon–5pm), the site of
a 15th-century Augustinian monastery.
Medieval artefacts discovered here are
displayed inside the unusual black-and-
white house, designed in 1939 for the
author Gunnar Gunnarsson. He later
gifted it to the Icelandic state to use as
a cultural centre and writers' retreat.
Klausturkaffi (see ③) here makes a
great lunch stop.

Skriðuklaustur's next-door neighbour, **Snæfellsstofa** ⑬ (tel: 470 0840;
www.vatnajokulsthjodgardur.is; daily
June–Aug 9am–5pm, May and Sept
10am–5pm, mid-Apr and Oct 10am–
4pm), is one of four visitor centres for

Vatnajökull National Park, with excellent
exhibitions on eastern Iceland's flora and
fauna and the nearby mountain **Snæfell**.

A kilometre up the road from the visitor centre, Route 910 launches itself
up the mountain in sharp switchbacks.
Just beyond the turn-off, look out for
Hengifoss ⑭, one of Iceland's highest
waterfalls at 128 metres (420ft), with
distinctive iron-red stripes cutting into
the cliff behind. A steep 2.5km (1.5-
mile) **hiking trail** leads up to it, passing
another lovely waterfall, **Litlanesfoss**,
with two distinct steps and flanked by
exceptional basalt columns.

After 25km (15.5 miles), turn right
onto Route 1, which brings you back
into Egilsstaðir.

Food and drink

① LANGABÚÐ CAFÉ

Búð 1, 765 Djúpivogur; tel: 478 8220;
www.langabud.is; daily 10am–6pm, Fri–
Sat also 9pm–midnight; $$
Located inside the cultural centre,
Langabúð café offers a variety of high-
quality homemade treats including soups,
sandwiches and cakes, as well as a selection
of Icelandic beers and spirits. Vegan and
gluten-free options are available.

② TÆRGESEN

Búðargata 4, 730 Reyðarfjörður;
tel: 470 5555; http://www.taergesen.com;
daily 10am–10pm; $$
Dating from around 1870 and located near
Reyðarfjörður harbour, Tærgesen serves up
traditional hearty fare in cosy surroundings,
with warm hospitality to match.

③ KLAUSTURKAFFI

Skriðuklaustur, 701 Egilsstaðir; tel: 471
2990; www.skriduklaustur.is; daily June–Aug
10am-6pm, May & Sept 11am–5pm, Apr
noon–4pm; $$
In Gunnar Gunnarsson's former dining room,
Klausturkaffi makes a great lunch stop.
There's a daily buffet, featuring local produce
like reindeer, Arctic char and blueberry ice
cream; and for the sweet-toothed, a cake
buffet with to-die-for skyr cake.

Whale–watching boats depart from Húsavík

THE NORTHEAST

The Arctic sea holds the remote fishing villages and wild shores of the northeast in its icy grip. The biggest pulls are Húsavík, Iceland's 'whale–watching capital'; and Jökulsárgljúfur, a spectacular river canyon created by glacial floods.

DISTANCE: 354km (224 miles)
TIME: Two to three days
START: Bustarfell
END: Goðafoss
POINTS TO NOTE: Pack a swimsuit for the swimming pool at Selárdalslaug. Húsavík's whale-watching operators offer 5–10% discounts for online bookings. If driving to Dettifoss from the north sounds too rough, the southern approach from Route 1 is on newly paved Route 862. Note that outside Húsavík there are very few independent eating options – some accommodation spots offer food – so bring provisions with you.

At the edge of the Arctic, the northeast is one of Iceland's most isolated areas, as obscure to most Reykjavíkers as it is to foreigners. Seabirds and driftwood from as far away as Siberia are strewn along the empty coastline, which is faithfully followed by the main road of the region, the partially unsurfaced Route 85.

VOPNAFJÖRÐUR

In some of Iceland's most barren landscape, between Egilsstaðir and Mývatn Route 85 branches off the Ring Road and climbs into the northeastern desert. In Hofsárdalur (follow Route 920, then Route 9143; signposted) is one of Iceland's best-preserved turf-roofed farmhouses, **Bustarfell ❶**, built in 1770 and now an excellent **folk museum** (tel: 844 1153; www.bustarfell.is; June–mid-Sept daily 10am–5pm) with a café.

From here, continue via Routes 920 and 917 to **Vopnafjörður ❷**, set in a picturesque location and backed by mountains. **Salmon rivers** tumble down from the heights – Britain's Prince Charles and former US president George Bush Sr have both fished here. The town has a poignant history as an emigration point – thousands of Icelanders sailed from Vopnafjörður to America and Canada, after the Askja eruption of 1875 made life intolerably hard. The hillsides around town are full of abandoned farms, the inspiration for Halldór Laxness's iconic novel *Independent People*.

Lush Ásbyrgi canyon

Head north out of town on Route 85, over the causeway and 5km (3 miles) on to the turn-off to sweet little geothermal swimming pool **Selárdalslaug** ❸ (May–Aug daily noon–10pm, Sept–Apr Tue–Fri 2–6pm, Sat–Sun noon–4pm), in a green, secluded valley.

COD COAST

Route 85 passes uneventful Bakkafjörður and continues to **Þórshöfn** ❹, where it's worth breaking your journey to admire the busy harbour. From Þórshöfn, the brave can take Route 869, which heads northeast past the airfield, becoming a dirt road as it enters windswept **Langanes** ❺, a peninsula whose marshy, cliff-bound expanses, only accessible by 4WD or on foot, are the last word in Icelandic isolation.

Sixty kilometres (37 miles) northwest of Þórshöfn is the flat, tundra-like peninsula of **Melrakkaslétta** ('fox plain'), where winds howl straight from the North Pole in winter. The coastline sup-

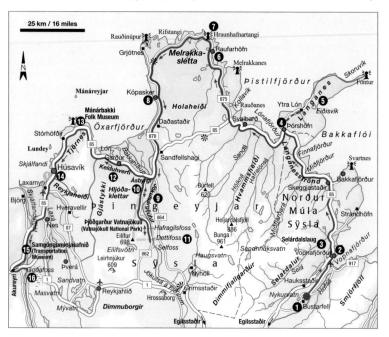

Purple lupins populate Vatnajökull

ports a good deal of birdlife, but there are only two human settlements (where you might stay to break up the long drive to Húsavík). The first is remote **Raufarhöfn ❻**, Iceland's most northerly village. Once it was one of the country's largest export harbours, during the herring boom of the 1940s and 50s; today just 173 people scrape a living here. On a hill overlooking the village are the basalt arches of the (unfinished) **Arctic Henge**, a large-scale sculpture inspired by mythology from the Eddic poem *Völuspá*.

Beyond Raufarhöfn, the northernmost part of mainland Iceland, **Hraunhafnartangi ❼**, is marked by a lighthouse – the Arctic Circle lies just 2.5km (1.5 miles) offshore.

On the other side of Melrakkaslétta, **Kópasker ❽**, with a population of 109, is another ghost town, unrecognisable from its herring-boom days. Today its biggest business is Fjallalamb, a lamb-processing factory with 20 full-time employees. In the village school, the **Earthquake Centre** (June–Aug daily 1–5pm; free) is an exhibition about local eruptions and seismic shake-ups, such as the 1976 quake that created two nearby lakes. At the edge of the village, a host of creepy scarecrows bids you adieu.

VATNAJÖKULL NATIONAL PARK: JÖKULSÁRGLJÚFUR

Ásbyrgi
The turn-off to one of Iceland's greatest natural attractions lies 40km (25 miles) south along Route 85. **Jökulsárgljúfur ❾**, the country's longest river canyon at 25km (16 miles), lies in a region of bleak beauty forming the northern section of the immense Vatnajökull National Park.

The great horseshoe-shaped canyon **Ásbyrgi ❿** sits at the turn-off. Sheltered green woodland of birch, willow and mountain ash covers the canyon bottom, surrounded by a curving wall of 100-metre (330ft) -high cliffs. Geologists believe the canyon was formed by two catastrophic *jökulhlaups* (glacial floods), caused by eruptions under faraway Vatnajökull icecap, 8–10,000 and 3,000 years ago. More romantically, Viking settlers believed it was a giant hoofprint made by Sleipnir, Odin's eight-legged horse.

Ásbyrgi visitor centre (daily mid-May–mid-Sept 9am–7pm, early May and late-Sept–Oct 10am–4pm, Nov–late Dec and mid Jan–Apr 11am–3pm), near the canyon's entrance, explores the history, geology and wildlife of Jökulsárgljúfur. It also has information on the area's many and varied hiking trails, from easy strolls to challenging paths and multiday hikes.

Towards Dettifoss
The rest of the park follows the powerful **Jökulsá á Fjöllum**, Iceland's second-longest river, south. Two dirt/gravel tracks open in summer and run the length of the river canyon on either bank (eastern 864 and western 862). Both are rough, jouncing 20kph (12mph)

rides all the way to Dettifoss – check with your car-hire company whether you are allowed to drive on them.

The western 862 runs across classic highland heather to **Vesturdalur**, with walking trails to **Hljóðaklettar** ('echoing rocks'), a tangle of fantastical basalt formations. Further on, the road heads to **Hólmatungur**, a lush stretch along the river canyon, before crossing a suddenly barren desert landscape to **Dettifoss** ⓫, Europe's most powerful waterfall. Five hundred cubic metres (17,700 cubic ft) of water spill over its ledges every second, and you can hear the thunderous drumming long before you see the hypnotic torrent.

Continue south to the Ring Road to cut directly west to Mývatn (see page 76); or return to Route 85 and head west towards Húsavík.

Formidable Dettifoss waterfall

HÚSAVÍK

Route 85 crosses the plain of **Kelduhverfi** ⓬, made up of sandy glacial outwash similar to the larger *sandur* in the south. This is the northern point of the great rift zone where Iceland pulls itself in two. At the top of the squat **Tjörnes** peninsula is **Mánárbakki Folk Museum** ⓭ (June–Aug daily 9am–6pm), a quirky collection of packaging, porcelain, paintings and postcards, amassed by weatherman Aðalgeir Egilsson.

Twenty-five kilometres (15.5 miles) south is the region's main town, pretty **Húsavík** ⓮ (population 2,200), with a glittering bay backed by snow-topped mountains and a busy harbour full of colourful fishing trawlers. After a long drive, it's worth staying overnight and going out to sea in the morning, followed by lunch at easygoing **Gamli Baukur** (see ⓵).

Whale watching

Húsavík is Iceland's 'whale-watching capital', thanks to its location on Skjálfandi Bay, a plankton- and fish-rich feeding ground that attracts migrating whales. The four local **whale-watching companies** – Gentle Giants (tel: 464 1500; www.gentlegiants.is); North Sailing (tel: 464 7272; www.northsailing.is); Húsavík Adventures (tel: 853 4205; husavikadventures.is); and Salka (tel: 464 3999; http://salkawhalewatching.is) – claim a 98 percent success rate for cetacean sightings, with the most commonly sighted species being

White-beaked dolphins usually travel in pods of five to 50 individuals

minke, humpback, white-beaked dolphins and harbour porpoises. Tours run March to November, up to seven times daily in July and August (less frequently at other times).

Bone up on whales beforehand at the excellent harbourside **Húsavík Whale Museum** (www.whalemuseum. is; June–July daily 8.30am–6.30pm, May and Sept daily 9am–6pm, Oct–Apr Mon–Fri 10am–4pm), with exhibits on whale species and biology, and the history of whaling in Iceland, plus an impressive gallery of whale skeletons.

Other sights in Húsavík

Two other museums are worth investigating. A prize exhibit at **Safnahúsið** (www.husmus.is; June–Sept daily 10am–6pm, Oct–May Mon–Fri 10am–4pm) is the polar bear that floated from Greenland to Grímsey island in 1973, only to be greeted by a bullet in the skull.

Centrally located, the **Exploration Museum** (www.explorationmuseum. com; daily June–Aug 2–6pm, Sept noon–3pm) celebrates human exploration, from prehistoric times to the space age. It includes photographs and artefacts from the Apollo Training Centre, near Húsavík, where US astronauts practised for their trip to the moon.

The town's unusual cross-shaped **church** was designed by the Icelandic architect Rögnvaldur Ólafsson and built in 1907 from Norwegian timber. It contains an impressive altarpiece, depicting Lazarus raised from the dead.

REJOINING THE RING ROAD

Still following Route 85 south out of Húsavík, after 35km (22 miles) you will come to the **Transportation Museum** ⑮ (Samgönguminjasafnið; www.ystafell.is; mid-May–Sept daily 10am–8pm) at Ystafell. Its unusual vehicles, collected by a local mechanic, include a Canadian military truck used to deliver milk and a giant snowmobile that functioned as a school bus.

As Route 85 rejoins the Ring Road, just to the east is the perfectly proportioned waterfall **Goðafoss** ⑯, the 'Waterfall of the Gods'. After Iceland converted to Christianity in the year 1000, law-speaker Þorgeir, returning from the momentous Alþingi where the decision was made, threw his pagan carvings into its waters.

From here, you can continue east to Lake Mývatn (see page 76) or head west for the big-city charms of Akureyri (see page 81).

Food and drink

① GAMLI BAUKUR

Hafnarstétt 9, Húsavík; tel: 464 2442; www.gamlibaukur.is; daily 9am–9pm; $$
Step off the whale-watching boat and into this lively bar-restaurant, built from driftwood and popular with both locals and visitors. The fish here is truly delicious and is served with creative sauces, including a tangy pesto.

Lake Mývatn

MÝVATN

Lovely Lake Mývatn is a premier wildlife habitat, with rich birdlife that wows even non-naturalists. Krafla volcano, the lake's moody next-door neighbour, advertises its presence with boiling mudpots, screaming chimneys, the stench of sulphur and smouldering black earth.

DISTANCE: Mývatn cycle ride: 34km (21 miles); Mývatn drive 32km (20 miles)
TIME: Two days
START & END: Reykjahlíð
POINTS TO NOTE: Make sure to bring binoculars on the cycle ride to see the birdlife, as well as insect repellent. Hire bicycles from Mývatn Activity (Reykjahlíð; tel: 899 4845; http://hike andbike.is). Rental hours are 9am–5pm daily: it's worth paying extra for a late (midnight) drop-off so you don't have to rush. It's also possible to cycle the Mývatn driving itinerary, although it's hillier and the gravel roads are hard going.

Mývatn ('Midge Lake') is Iceland's fourth largest lake at 37 sq km (14 sq miles), but has an average depth of just 2 metres (7ft), allowing the sun's rays to thoroughly warm the water. The shallow, sheltered coves, luxurious heat and summer surfeit of tiny midges make the wetlands a favourite waterfowl breeding and feeding ground, especially for ducks.

The lake and Laxá river form a highly important national conservation area, a veritable oasis on the fringes of Iceland's bleak northern deserts.

REYKJAHLÍÐ

Tiny **Reykjahlíð** ❶ at the northeast corner of Lake Mývatn has become the main service centre of the area (Skútustaðir, on the southern shore, also has good facilities). The **visitors' centre** (tel: 464 4460) has good information on Mývatn's unique ecosystem and hikes in the area.

The main sight in the village is the **church**, surrounded by hardened lava. In 1729, a major eruption of Leirhnjúkur crater sent lava streaming down to Reykjahlíð, obliterating its farms and buildings. Miraculously, it parted at the church door, flowing around the building. The current church was rebuilt in 1972, on the site of the original.

CYCLE CIRCUIT AROUND THE LAKE

It's possible to drive around Lake Mývatn, taking in the main sights, but you get a

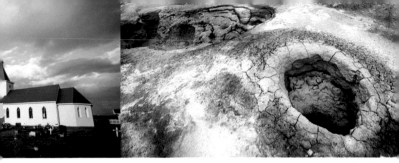

Reykjahlíð church

Mudpot at Krafla caldera

much better appreciation of its scale, beauty and fragility on a satisfying cycle around the flat 34km (21 mile) road. An anticlockwise route is outlined below.

Western shore

Heading north out of Reykjahlíð, Route 1 passes the airfield and crosses the 1720s lava flow **Eldhraun** ('fire lava'), before turning left down the western side of the lake, where you quickly reach the **conservation area**. This is the main breeding ground for the lake's summer migrants, attracted by the warm shallow water, plentiful food and nesting space. During the nesting season (15 May–20 July), the shoreline is off-limits.

For more information on birdlife, turn left onto **Neslandatangi peninsula** and head to **Sigurgeir Bird Museum ❷** (Fuglasafn Sigurgeirs; www.fuglasafn.is; daily mid-May–end May noon–5pm, June–Aug 9am–6pm, Sept–Oct noon–5pm, Nov–mid-May 2–4pm). The museum is a tribute to avid bird- and egg-collector Sigurgeir, incorporating his private collection and containing an example of almost every species of Icelandic bird.

The calm **museum café**, see ❶, overlooks the lake, and there are bird hides nearby.

South of the conservation area, there are fantastic views from the peak of **Vindbelgjarfjall ❸** (530 metres/1,735ft) – allow two hours to climb up and back down the fairly steep path. South again, Route 1 crosses the River Laxá, full of salmon, brown trout and Arctic char, before it peels away west.

Southern shore

You should turn east onto Route 848, which runs to Mývatn's secondary service centre, **Skútustaðir ❹**, 4km (2.5 miles) away, with a café serving

Grjótagjá thermal spring

light lunches. An easy hour-long path leads around the **Skútustaðagígar pseudocraters** ❺, formed 2,300 years ago when molten lava ran over the marsh. The water beneath boiled and burst up through the lava sheet, forming what look like mini volcanic cones.

Eastern shore

Rounding the southeastern corner of the lake, you come to one of the most sheltered and relaxing spots on the lakeside. **Höfði** ❻ is a forested promontory that has been turned into a nature reserve (small admission fee), with paths running through flower-covered lava outcrops and forests of birch trees.

Just north of Höfði, a turn-off to the right leads to enchanting **Dimmuborgir** ❼ ('black castles'), a 2,000-year-old field of contorted volcanic pillars. Visitors can wander among haunting arches, caves and natural tunnels – the area is very fragile, so stick to paths. The most famous formation is **Kirkjan** (the Church), a cave resembling the doorway of a Gothic cathedral. A helpful **visitor centre** (June–Aug daily 9am–10pm) offers guided walks. Dimmuborgir skirts the edge of the vast tephra cone **Hverfell** – a steep path runs up the side. Those who climb it are rewarded with sweeping views of Mývatn.

En route back to Reykjahlíð, reward yourself for a long day's pedal with home-made ice-cream at the unique **Vogafjós** (see ❷). The track on the other side of the road from the café leads to **Grjótagjá** ❽, about 1km (0.5 miles) away. *Game of*

Thrones fans will recognise this underground hot spring as the place where Jon Snow and Ygritte had their first clinch. The green waters are scalding below the surface, so swimming is forbidden.

Rejoin the road. Two kilometres (1 mile) north, turn left at the junction with Route 1 to return to Reykjahlíð.

NÁMAFJALL AND HVERIR

Spend the second day in Mývatn taking in the amazing geothermal sights north-east of the lake by car. A kilometre or two east of Reykjahlíð on Route 1, the landscape becomes a desolate, sandy plain of mixed orange and brown hues known as **Bjarnarflag** ❾. In this bleak landscape, enterprising Icelanders have harvested microscopic fossils (diatoms); made bricks from the endless tephra; and even done a bit of cooking. A local speciality, *hverabrauð* (hot-spring bread), is still baked here using geothermal heat. Sweet, heavy rye dough is poured into tins, which are lowered into the hot ground, covered by metal sheets, and left to bake for 24 hours.

Mývatn Nature Baths

Geothermally heated water from the Bjarnarflag borehole fills **Mývatn Nature Baths** ❿ (Jarðböðin; www.myvatnnaturebaths.is; daily mid-May–Sept 9am–midnight, Oct–mid-May noon–10pm), the north's answer to the Blue Lagoon, lying just off the Ring Road. Here you can soothe yesterday's aching cycling mus-

The moon-like landscape and steaming mud pits of Hverir

cles in its 38–40° waters, which contain a mix of skin-softening minerals and silicates. In addition to the main pool, there are hot-pots and two steam saunas. Have lunch at **Kvika**, see ❸ – note that this is the only restaurant on today's route.

Námafjall

As Route 1 climbs over the ridge of **Námafjall** ⓫, an overwhelming eggy stench greets travellers. From the 14th to the 19th century, sulphur mined here was sent to Europe, to be made into the gunpowder that kept the world's wars rolling. The Námafjall geothermal field, located plumb on the Mid-Atlantic Ridge, has had 14 boreholes sunk into it over the past 50 years, the highest recorded temperature being 320°C (608°F) at a depth of 1.8km (1 mile). At the pass is a parking area with views over the lake.

Hverir

On the other side of the ridge is **Hverir** ⓬, one of Iceland's most infernal and fascinating sights. Walkways run across the multicoloured clay of this highly active high-temperature area, past dozens of bubbling mud pits and screaming fumaroles. The surface crust here is particularly thin: keep well within the marked paths.

KRAFLA

Just east past Hverir, take Route 863 north towards the **Krafla caldera**. A magma chamber 3–8km (2–5 miles) beneath Krafla is the source of the lively

volcanic activity around Mývatn, with eruptions occurring on and off for 3,000 years. Molten rock builds up in the chamber, pushing the earth's surface upwards, before it bursts out in lava flows, allowing the surface to sink again. The most recent activity was the 'Krafla Fires', which began in 1975 with earthquakes, fissuring and lava fountains and continued for a decade, leaving the ground still scorched and steaming today.

The Fires threatened **Krafla geothermal power plant** ⓭, but stopped

Birds of Mývatn

Around 115 species of birds have been recorded around Lake Mývatn and the Laxá River. Most are summer migrants, arriving from late April onwards. Fourteen species of ducks breed here at a density unmatched anywhere else in the world – tens of thousands waddle in the warm water, eating midges and nesting in the grasses around the water's edge.

The most common varieties are the tufted duck, scaup, wigeon, teal and red-breasted merganser. Harlequin ducks live on the river in large numbers, and the common scoter, a diving breed, is widely seen on the west side of the lake. Barrow's goldeneye, one of the few birds to overwinter at Mývatn, is only found here and in North America. In the Rockies, where the species originates, the birds lay their eggs in holes in tree trunks; here, they lay them in holes in the lava.

Charming Siglufjörður

just short; you can learn more about living and working on top of a volcanic timebomb at the plant's **visitor center** (June–mid-Sept daily 10am–5pm).

Leirhnjúkur and Víti

Past the power plant, a kilometre-long track leads from a car park up to **Leirhnjúkur** ⑭, a colourful lavafield formed in the 1720s and given fresh life by the Krafla Fires. A path passes a large sulphur-encrusted mud-hole, before winding around cinder-like mounds and smoking black fissures. This whole lifeless, primeval area gives as good a glimpse of the freshly formed earth as you're likely to get.

Dirt road 863 ends at a second car park, 1km (0.5 miles) further along, at the base of **Víti** ⑮ ('hell'), a dingey-brown explosion crater, filled with cold floodwater. Víti's huge size, the strange blue tint to the water and the sheer drop down from the rim make it an eerie sight. A walking trail leads around the crater edge.

Víti is close to **Mount Krafla** ⑯ itself, which, far from being a classic volcanic cone, is the rim of a larger caldera that has been worn and exploded almost beyond recognition.

Back to Reykjahlíð

From here, return the way you came to Reykjahlíð. Round off the day with an evening sightseeing flight (tel 464 4400; www.myflug.is) from the airstrip, a fantastic way to get an overall sense of this volcanic landscape. Flights operate on request May to September.

Food and drink

① SIGURGEIR BIRD MUSEUM CAFÉ

660 Mývatn; www.fuglasafn.is; daily mid-May noon–5pm, June–Aug 9am–6pm, Sept–Oct noon–5pm, Nov–mid-May 2–4pm; $

Floor-to-ceiling windows in the dining room look out over the lake – rich in bird life, naturally – and you can eat outdoors in summer. The traditional Icelandic fare served here includes rye bread with smoked brown trout, flatbread with smoked lamb and baked waffles.

② VOGAFJÓS

660 Mývatn; tel: 464 3800; www.vogafjos. is; June–Aug daily 7.30am–11pm, Sept daily 10am–10pm, times vary in winter; $$$

Farm-to-table has a very literal meaning at Vogafjós – or the Cowshed Café – where you can watch cows being milked (at 7.30am and 5.30pm) while you eat farm-made cheese and ice cream. It's a great place for lunch, or an excellent evening meal made with fresh-as-can-be ingredients.

③ KVIKA RESTAURANT

Mývatn Nature Baths, Jarðbaðshólar; tel: 464 4411; www.myvatnnaturebaths.is; daily mid-May–Sept 9am–midnight, Oct–mid-May noon–10pm; $–$$

The restaurant at Mývatn Nature Baths is large and modern, with a sunny terrace.

Meeting folklore figures in Akureyri

AKUREYRI & AROUND

Akureyri, the capital of the north, is an attractive town, with snowcapped mountains and a sheltering fjord that protect it from Arctic winds. Fishing villages and interesting islands steeped in history lie on and off Tröllaskagi peninsula.

DISTANCE: Akureyri town walk: 5km (3 miles); Tröllaskagi peninsula drive: 140km (87 miles)
TIME: Two days
START: Akureyri port
END: Sauðárkrókur
POINTS TO NOTE: Akureyri's buses are all free: you could pick up a schedule from the tourist office and hop on a bus if you fancy a change from walking around town. Bring a swimsuit if you fancy a swim at the end of your walk. For the Tröllaskagi drive, make sure to book ahead online for the Beer Spa (www.bjorbodin.com).

By Icelandic standards, Akureyri is a thriving metropolis. It is the country's second 'city', although its 18,200-strong population makes it more of a provincial town.

Akureyri's gentle charms and historic buildings can be explored in a day. Good restaurants, shops and hotels make the town an excellent base for exploring Eyjafjörður and Tröllaskagi peninsula, and a launchpad for bus and boat trips further afield. This is also a great area to take in the northern lights (see page 83).

AKUREYRI

Akureyri ❶ enjoys a spectacular setting, alongside sparkling Eyjafjörður, with a backdrop of sheer granite snow-tipped mountains. Despite being only 100km (60 miles) from the Arctic Circle, it enjoys some of the country's warmest weather, bringing the flowers, the café tables and the people out into the pedestrianised streets in summer.

At the port

Akureyri stretches in a long, narrow ribbon by the water, from the airport in the south to the residential Síðuhverfi district 10km (6 miles) to the north; however its shopping centre and old town are compact enough to explore on foot. The fjordside **port ❹** usually contains picturesque trawlers or an impressive cruise ship. Several companies here also offer three-hour **whale-watching**

trips – humpbacks and minkes are often seen in Eyjafjörður, which is Iceland's longest, deepest fjord.

Hof Culture Centre 🅱 contains the town's **tourist office** (Strandgata 12; tel: 450 1050; www.visitakureyri.is; June–mid-Sept daily 8am–6.30pm, late May and late Sept Mon–Fri 8am–5pm, Sat–Sun 8am–4pm, Oct–mid-May Mon–Fri 8am–4pm), where you can pick up information or book trips.

The city centre

Cross multi-laned Glerárgata at the traffic lights and head up Strandgata, past the cinema on your left, to contrary Ráðhústorg – the 'Town Hall Square' has a circular centre, and the proposed town hall was never built! Walking clockwise around the edge, you will pass Skipagata, before reaching **Hafnarstræti** 🅲, the partly pedestrianised main shopping street. This is where the hustle and bustle (such as it is) of this small town's life takes place – take some time to explore the shops and pick up some souvenirs.

Hafnarstræti forms a crossroad with Kaupvangsstræti, once the most hardworking street in town, with factories, abattoirs, laundries and a cornmill. Today it has a more cultured feel: **Akureyri Art Museum** 🅳 (www.listak.is; due to reopen summer 2018), just up the hill on your right, has changing exhibitions of modern art.

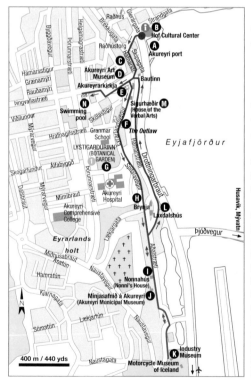

Colourful blooms in Akureyri Botanical Gardens

At the crossroad, your eyes will inevitably be drawn upwards to the twin steeples of **Akureyrarkirkja** **Ⓔ**, especially dramatic when spotlit against the night sky. This eye-catching building was designed by architect Guðjón Samúelsson, who also designed Hallgrímskirkja in Reykjavík. It's worth climbing the 102 steps for fjord views. Inside the church, the middle stained-glass window in the choir comes from the original Coventry cathedral in the UK. It was removed at the start of World War II, before the cathedral was destroyed by bombs, and rescued from a London antique shop. Other notable features are the huge organ with 3,300 pipes, and the votive ship hanging from the ceiling.

The Botanical Gardens

Follow the diagonal path round the back of the church to Eyrarlandsvegur, turning left onto the street. After 200 metres/yds, look for Einar Jónsson's sculpture *The Outlaw* **Ⓕ**, opposite the Catholic church, which depicts Fjalla-Eyvindur ('Mountain-Eyvind') and his wife Halla, who spent 20 years as outlaws in the mountains.

You next pass the very fetching white **schoolhouse**, built in 1904, and still used as a grammar school today, before reaching another of the town's jewels. The **Botanical Gardens** **Ⓖ** (Lystigarðurinn; Eyrarlandsvegur; www.lystigardur.akureyri.is; June–Sept Mon–Fri 8am–10pm, Sat–Sun 9am–10pm; free) are famed for their 7,000 species of local and foreign flowers, from southern Europe, Africa, South America and Australasia, all blooming merrily in Akureyri's warm microclimate. They are the perfect place to relax on a sunny day: stop at lovely **Café Laut** (see **①**), by the top entrance, for a light lunch.

The northern lights

The bewitching aurora borealis, commonly known as the northern lights, flashes, flickers and pulses across the winter sky like silent fireworks. This eerie green lightshow, sometimes tinged with purples, pinks and reds, has been the source of many a high-latitude superstition: the Vikings, for example, believed it was the Valkyries riding across the sky. The scientific explanation is no less astonishing. The lights are actually caused by streams of charged particles – 'solar wind' – that flare into space from our sun. When the wind comes into contact with the Earth's magnetic field, it is drawn towards the poles, where its electrical charge agitates particles of oxygen and nitrogen in the atmosphere, making them glow.

In Iceland, the lights can be seen between September/October and March/April, with midnight being the most likely time to see them... but as with all natural phenomena, there's no timetable and sightings are not guaranteed. Choose a cold, clear, moonless night; then look heavenwards and hope.

Akureyrarkirkja church, illuminated against the night sky

The old town

After admiring the gardens, leave by the gate you came in at. Continue along Eyrarlandsvegur for about 80 metres/yds, then turn left onto Spitalvegur. You are now entering the **old town** area, with some fine buildings in the so-called Icelandic frame-house tradition – they look a little like Swiss chalets. The last one was built in 1911, when other styles came into vogue, including the use of metal sidings pressed into a brick pattern and painted over to look like stone and mortar.

At the very bottom of the hill, take a quick left to **Aðalstræti**, a leafy street with historic houses and museums. Across the street is **Brynja** ❽, said to sell the best ice cream in Iceland. Turn right and walk down Aðalstræti, where you'll pass a charming row of **19th century houses**. Just after the waterfront opens up, at Aðalstræti 54 you can visit **Nonni's House** ❾ (Nonnahús; www.

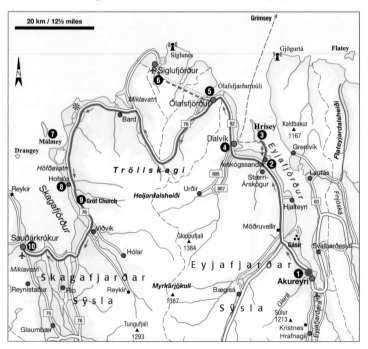

nonni.is; June–Aug daily 10am–5pm, Sept–Oct Thu–Sun 10am–5pm), one of the most interesting of Akureyri's old buildings. This tiny, black, wood construction was the home of Reverend Jón Sveinsson, nicknamed Nonni, whose children's books were translated into 40 languages and are still well loved in Iceland and continental Europe.

Nearby, **Akureyri Municipal Museum** ❶ (Minjasafnið á Akureyri; Aðalstræti 58; www.minjasafnid.is; daily June–Sept 10am–5pm, Oct–May 1–4pm) has a wide collection of everyday items, from old farming tools to milk cartons, as well as some excellent 19th-century photographs. The church here is still used for weddings.

Industry and motorbikes

At the very end of this picturesque street and a tad beyond are two specialist museums, the **Industry Museum** ❶ (Iðnaðarsafnið; Eyjafjarðarbraut vestri; www.idnadarsafnid.is; June–mid-Sept daily 10am–5pm, mid-Sept–May Sat 2–4pm), detailing Akureyri's 20th-century industrial heritage; and the **Motorcycle Museum of Iceland** (Mótorhjólasafn Íslands; Krókeyri 2; www.motorhjolasafn.is; mid-May–Aug daily 11am–5pm, Sept–mid-May Sat 3–7pm), which covers the 100-year-old history of Icelandic motorbikes.

Back to town

Retrace your steps down Aðalstræti, turning right onto Hafnarstræti. A short distance along, on the left with a rowan tree in the garden, is Akureyri's oldest house, **Laxdalshús** ❶, built in 1795. Hafnarstræti leads you on a pleasant 2km (1.2 mile) stroll back to town, past more historic buildings, including the **old schoolhouse** at 53; the '**people's house**' at 57, where Akureyri residents gathered for fundraisers, dancing, boxing demonstrations and films; and the **House of the Verbal Arts** ❶ (Sigurhæðir), with a waterfall flowing down the hill in front. The latter was the home of one of Iceland's most revered poets and dramatists, Mattías Jochumsson (1835–1920), who wrote the lyrics for Iceland's national anthem, Lofsöngur, first sung on the 1,000th anniversary of the settlement of Iceland.

Back at the foot of Akureyrarkirkja, turn left up Kaupvangsstræti, which becomes Þingvallastræti. Akureyri's **swimming pool** ❶ (Þingvallastræti 2; tel: 461 4455; Mon–Fri 6.45am–9pm, Sat & Sun 9am–6.30pm) is one of the best in the country, with two outdoor pools, an indoor pool, two waterslides, hot tubs, a steam room and sauna. In summer, there are extra distractions for children, including mini-golf and electric cars.

If you don't feel like a swim, stop for afternoon tea at an Akureyri institution, **Bautinn**, at the crossroads, whose glassed-in conservatory is a good place to watch Akureyri's world go by; or at **Bláa Kannan**, another 19th-century beauty, painted royal-blue with bright red turrets.

TRÖLLASKAGI PENINSULA

Route 82 north from Akureyri brings you to **Árskógssandur ❷**, 35km (22 miles) away, where you can make the joyful 15-minute sailing to the sparsely inhabited island of Hrísey – ferries depart every two hours. Aim to catch the 7.20am or 9am ferry, depending on whether you want to go for a walk on the island.

Hrísey Island

Hrísey ❸ (population 153), the second largest island after Heimaey in the Vestmannaeyjar, is a lovely spot on a sunny day. As you step off the ferry, you are generally greeted by an old tractor and haycart that can take you on a 40-minute **island tour** (tel: 695 0077).

The north of the island is private property, but there are three **marked walking trails**, from 2.3km (1.4 mile) to 5km (3 miles) long, across the flat southern moorlands, covered in pretty purple heather and full of birdlife – there are around 40 species on the island. Hrísey is particularly famous for its fearless ptarmigan, which appears on its coat of arms; their numbers swell in autumn, and they can often be seen waddling down the streets.

The oldest house is **Hús Hákarla-Jörundar** (tel: 695 0077; June–Aug daily 1–5pm), built from the timber of Norwegian ships abandoned at Hrísey. It contains the tourist office, and an exhibition on shark-fishing.

Head back on the 1pm ferry.

To Dalvík

Back on the mainland, local craft brewery Kaldi opened **Bjórböðin Beer Spa** (Ægisgata 31; tel: 414 2828, 699 0715; www.bjorbodin.com; Mon–Thu 3–7pm, Fri & Sat 11am–9pm, Sun

> ## Grímsey
>
> The Arctic Circle runs through the centre of Grímsey (pop. 67): once you've crossed it, you can buy yourself a commemorative certificate from Gallerí Sól, by the harbour. The island's community centre honours Daniel Willard Fiske, a 19th-century American chess champion who had read about the island's love for the game. He gave every home a marble chessboard, and left money that was used to build the school and library. Locals still celebrate his birthday on 11 November.
>
> Grímsey is well known for its extensive birdlife – the craggy cliffs on the north and east of the island are home to about 60 species, including puffins, kittiwakes and razorbills.
>
> In summer, you can sail to Grímsey and back, with four or five hours on the island, on Monday, Wednesday, Friday and Sunday – the ferry leaves Dalvík at 9am and gets back at 8pm. The new 6.5-hour Arctic Circle Express tour (http://ambassador.is; June–Aug) from Akureyri can also whizz you there; or take one of the regular 30-minute flights (see www.flugfelag.is) to/from Akureyri.

Grímsey lighthouse

noon–7pm) in Árskógssandur in 2017, where you can unwind in a big tub filled with (non-drinkable) young, hoppy beer. You can also taste the microbrewery's creations at the spa bar – for example, Stinnings Kaldi, which is given its liquorice flavour by angelica gathered on Hrísey – although you'll need someone else to drive afterwards! There are also plenty of beer-themed food goodies on the restaurant menu.

Continue on Route 82 to **Dalvík** ❹ (population 1,300). This fishing village was rebuilt after an earthquake demolished half its old buildings in 1934, but the harbourfront is still attractive. Its unusual little museum **Byggðasafnið Hvoll** (Karlsbraut; June–mid-Aug daily 11am–6pm, mid-Aug–May Sat 2–5pm) has a room containing photos and possessions belonging to local personality Jóhann Pétursson (1913–84), Iceland's tallest man, who stood an impressive 2.34 metres (7ft 8in) tall. Dalvík-based company Arctic Sea Tours (tel: 771 7600; www.arcticseatours. is) is a more peaceful **whale-watching** alternative to the scrum at Húsavík.

If you have a day or two to spare, and want to say you've crossed the Arctic Circle, the ferry over to **Grímsey** (see box) departs from Dalvík.

North to Siglufjörður

North of Dalvík, a 3.5km (2-mile) one-lane tunnel dives through the mountainside to **Ólafsfjörður** ❺, a fishing village of 796 people nestled amongst a ring of snow-capped, 1,200-metre (3,900ft) -high peaks. Despite its dramatic setting, it has little more of interest than fishing boats and factories.

Héðinsfjörður Tunnel carries Route 76 to the attractive town of **Siglufjörður** ❻, amid a range of glaciated mountains. The town's current population of 1,200 is its lowest in recent history, but a generation ago this was the home of the herring industry and 10,000 seasonal workers. The award-winning **Herring Era Museum** (Síldarminjasafn Íslands; www. sild.is; daily June–Aug 10am–6pm, May and Sept 1–5pm) traces the town's glory days in five historical buildings by the harbour, including the old shipyard, boathouse and slipway. It's an atmospheric spot, and feels as though the herring workers have just stepped out.

Ptarmigan turn almost totally white in winter

The musical might enjoy Siglufjörður's little **Folk Music Center** (Þjóðlagasetur sr.; www.folkmusik.is; June–Aug daily noon–6pm), in the house of Reverend Bjarni Þorsteinsson, an avid 19th-century collector of folk music. You can see traditional instruments like the langspil, and hear recordings of Iceland's epic chanted poetry (*rímur*) and eerie five-tone harmonies (*tvísöngur*). **Kaffi Rauðka** (see ②) at the harbour is the town's lively summer café, where all the action is on sunny days.

South to Sauðárkrókur

Taking Route 76 north from Siglufjörður brings you around the headland until you're heading south again into Skagafjörður. You may find your eyes drawn to the island of **Málmey** ❼, with cliffs rising at either end, which was inhabited until 1950 when a fire destroyed its single farmhouse.

Next is the little fishing village of **Hofsós** ❽, containing the **Icelandic Emigration Centre** (Vesturfarasetrið; www.hofsos.is; June–Aug daily 11am–6pm). If you think you are of Icelandic descent, this is the place to come to try to trace your roots. It is not just for genealogists, though – four truly fascinating exhibitions tell the story of the 16,000–20,000 Icelanders who emigrated west to the New World between 1850 and 1914.

Behind the museum, you can walk over a little white bridge onto Suður-braut, where after 400 metres (440yds) you reach the fabulous fjordside **swimming pool** (tel: 455 6070; www.facebook.com/sundlauginhofsosi; June–Aug daily 7am–9pm, Sept–May Mon–Fri 7am–1pm, 5.15–8.15pm, Sat–Sun 11am–3pm), one of Iceland's finest: it's not uncommon to see whales swim past as you're doing your lengths.

Back in the car, keep heading south, passing the oldest church in Iceland at **Gröf** ❾, then turn west onto Route 75, along bridges, beaches and black-sand marshland at the wide end of the fjord, to **Sauðárkrókur** ❿.

Food and drink

❶ CAFÉ LAUT

Eyrarlandsvegur 30, Akureyri; tel: 461 4601; late May–Sept daily 10am–8pm; $
This lovely wooden summer café inside the Botanical Gardens is bright, airy and almost church-like. It sells light meals (soup, salad, sandwiches, pasta, cakes), best eaten at the outdoor seating while soaking up the sun.

❷ KAFFI RAUÐKA

Gránugata 19, Siglufjörður; tel: 461 7734; www.hannesboy.is; June–Aug 11.30am–5pm; $$
In a bright red renovated warehouse by the harbour, Kaffi Rauðka is the place to be in summer. The menu is designed to suit all tastes, ranging from plokkfiskur (fish stew) to paninis, and frequent live music helps it all go down.

Drangey island

THE NORTHWEST

*A trip to Drangey and a wild ride down a turbulent glacial river
are options on this route. Otherwise Skagi and Vatnsnes peninsulas
lack high drama, but reward the patient with basalt rock formations,
throngs of seabirds and seals, and haunting saga tales.*

DISTANCE: 252km (157 miles)
TIME: One or one and a half days
START: Sauðárkrókur
END: Hvammstangi
POINTS TO NOTE: You can do this route in one long day without rafting, or one and a half days including a white-water trip, staying overnight in Varmahlíð.

Iceland's northwest may lack the breathtaking glaciers of the south and the drama of the wiggling West Fjords, but the fact that the region has been largely bypassed by tourism will appeal to many a traveller.

SAUÐÁRKRÓKUR AND AROUND

Sauðárkrókur ❶, settled by Hebridean Scots, has a population of about 2,500, making it second in size to Akureyri on the north coast. It has hotels, restaurants, a swimming pool and cinema.

Drangey island

Fifteen kilometres (9 miles) due north on unmade Route 748 is the farm **Reykir ❷**, from where three-hour boat trips to **Drangey island ❸** (tel: 821 0090; www.drangey.net; 20 May–20 Aug) depart at 10am in summer. It's a beautiful spot, steeped in saga history: the cursed hero Grettir the Strong hid on Drangey as an outlaw for the last three years of his life. Today the sheer-sided island is rich in birdlife, a nesting colony for thousands of puffins, fulmar, gannets, guillemots, kittiwakes and shearwaters. Climbing its vertical sides, with the help of ropes and handrails drilled into the rock, is not for the faint hearted. Get to Reykir early if you want to bathe in the two hotpots – **Grettislaug** and **Jarlslaug** – built over a natural hot pool and with glorious sea and mountain views.

Sauðárkrókur

Return to Sauðárkrókur for lunch – the bakery, **Sauðárkróksbakarí** (see ①), makes a great stop. If you can't make it to Drangey, you can experience the island's puffins via virtual reality at **Puffin and Friends** (Aðalgata 24; www.puffinandfriends.com; June–Sept daily 10am–6pm). Opened in 2017, this exhibition about the northern lights and Ice-

Turf farmhouse museum, Glaumbær

landic birdlife, whales, seals and polar bears exploits stunning cinematography.

Then, if you've been intrigued by the fish-leather clothing and salmon hand-

bags for sale around Iceland, visit the only **fish-leather tannery** in Europe at the eastern end of town: buy leather or arrange a tour at the **visitor centre** (Borgarmýri 5;

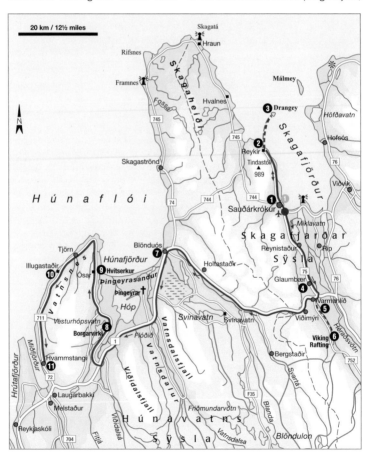

Hvítserkur troll-cow

Fish leather comes in an array of colours

www.facebook.com/tanneryvisitorcenter;
Mid-May–mid-Sept Mon–Fri 8am–4pm,
Sat–Sun 8am–noon, mid-Sept–mid-May
Mon–Fri 11am–4pm).

Glaumbær
A 15-minute drive south on Route 75
is **Glaumbær** ❹, a finely maintained
turf farmhouse museum (mid-May–
mid-Sept daily 9am–6pm, Apr–mid-
May and mid-Sept–mid-Oct Mon–Fri
10am–4pm), whose wood-framed buildings are insulated by thick turf walls
and roofs. **Áshús**, a house built in the
19th-century style that supplanted the
turf house, contains a coffee-shop that
also serves Icelandic pancakes.

Varmahlíð
Nine kilometres (5.5 miles) south of
Glaumbær, **Varmahlíð** ❺ is a small service village with a bank, two hotels, a
tourist office and swimming pool.

The rivers south of town are Iceland's
best for white-water rafting. Adventure
enthusiasts should seek out **Viking
Rafting** ❻ (tel: 823 8300; http://viking
rafting.is), located 15km (9 miles) south
of Varmahlíð on route 752, who operate
rafting trips on the beautiful glacial rivers Jökulsá Vestari and Jökulsá Austari,
lasting three to six hours. Stay overnight
at Varmahlíð and set off at 9am, or book
a 3pm rafting trip.

About 5km (3 miles) west of Varmahlíð, on a dirt track signposted off
Route 1, is **Víðimýrarkirkja**, one of six
turf churches remaining in Iceland.

WEST TO VATNSNES PENINSULA

If you choose to skip the rafting, the 50km
(30-mile) drive to **Blönduós** ❼ is uneventful, as is the town itself. Stop for a quick
driving break, before plunging on to the
turn-off north onto Route 716, then 717,
to **Borgarvirki** ❽, site of a natural basalt
fortress, used for defensive purposes during the bloody civil wars of the Sturlung
Age. From here, there is an 8km (5-mile)
stretch of bad road before you meet Route
711, which leads you in a 55km (34 mile)
loop around the Vatnsnes peninsula.

A highlight is the great stone troll-cow,
Hvítserkur ❾ – frozen by the sun while
drinking sea water, or so it is said – just off
the coast at Ósar. There's a seal-watching
hide (open from 20 June) at **Illugastaðir**
❿, site of a famous murder, leading to the
last public execution in Iceland (1830). At
Hvammstangi ⓫, a seal exhibition and
seal-watching trips are on offer at the **Icelandic Seal Center** (Brekkugata 2; www.
selasetur.is; June–Aug daily 9am–7pm,
May & Sept daily 9am–4pm, Oct–May
Mon–Fri 10am–3pm).

West Fjords Heritage Museum

THE WEST FJORDS

The wild West Fjords form a world of their own – remote, inaccessible, with a raw and jagged beauty that moves the soul. Bewitching mountains, waterfalls, fjords, beaches and bird cliffs take centre stage, with tiny villages dotting the landscape like an afterthought.

DISTANCE: 555km (345 miles)
TIME: Three days
START: Sheep Farming Museum, Sævangur
END: Flatey
POINTS TO NOTE: Distances are huge, villages are far-spaced, roads are sometimes poor and many places close outside the main summer season – it's best to take your time and keep emergency snacks and supplies in the car.

Many people scoot round the Ring Road, omitting the West Fjords entirely – yet it is one of the most scenic parts of Iceland, with dizzying views around every hairpin turn, some of the best hiking and millions of sea birds. The ratio of gravel to tarmac roads is about 50:50 on the peninsula, although main roads are mostly surfaced; however, sandwiched between the sea and sheer mountainsides, they wiggle around every fjord, making the going slow – and nightmarish for anyone with car sickness.

HÓLMAVÍK

The **Sheep Farming Museum ❶** (Sauð-fjársetur á Ströndum; www.strandir.is/saudfjarsetur/enska-index.htm; June–Aug daily 10am–6pm), at **Sævangur** on Route 68, is an unexpectedly interesting exhibition about Icelandic sheep farming in this remote region, with the opportunity to bottle-feed lambs, and a café selling pancakes.

Twelve kilometres (7.5 miles) north, **Hólmavík ❷** is the biggest settlement on the Strandir coast, with 336 people. Casting a spell on the town, the **Museum of Icelandic Sorcery & Witchcraft** (Galdrasýningar; www.galdrasyning.is; daily 11am–7pm) explores Iceland's gruesome 17th-century 'Brennuöld' (Burning Age), when 20 Icelanders were burned at the stake for practising black magic. Stop for an early lunch at **Café Riis** (see ❶), or take a picnic lunch for the journey.

TO ÍSAFJÖRÐUR

Continue west on Route 61. The road runs through a green river valley,

Ísafjörður is located on a spit of land, surrounded by water

rising over the starkly beautiful, water-drenched high heathland **Steingrimsfjörðurheiði**, before dropping back down. Near the bottom, Route 635 turns off north, faltering away at the foot of **Drangajökull**, the northernmost Icelandic ice cap. At the head of **Kaldalón glacial lagoon ❸**, 25km (15.5 miles) along Route 635, a **walking trail** (1.5 hours) leads to the edge of the glacier.

If you don't want to visit the lagoon, continue on Route 61 to sea level and the start of a seemingly endless series of fjords that lie between you and the main town of Ísafjörður, 175km (109 miles) away. From near to far, the bigger ones are: (confusingly) Ísafjörður, Reykjarfjörður, Mjóifjörður, Skötufjörður, Hestfjörður, Seyðisfjörður, Álftafjörður and Skutulsfjörður.

Reykjanes ❹, a former school, sits between the first two fjords, and is worth a stop for its heated **outdoor pool** – the longest in Iceland, thanks to a measuring mix-up. On Álftafjörður ('Swan Fjord'), **Súðavík ❺** has a community-run **Arctic Fox Center** (www.melrakki.is; June–Aug daily 9am–6pm, May and Sept daily 10am–4pm, Oct–Apr Mon–Fri 10am–2pm), with a permanent exhibition about one of Iceland's few land mammals, and two orphaned foxes called Ingi and Móri. Once hunted for their fur, Arctic foxes are still culled in Iceland to protect livestock, but are a protected species in this region.

ÍSAFJÖRÐUR AND AROUND

The only town of any real size in the whole of the West Fjords is **Ísafjörður ❻**, the region's friendly capital, with 2,600 people, a swimming pool, cinema and several restaurants and hotels (it makes sense to overnight here). Fishermen share the deep harbour with frequent summer cruise ships.

The town's oldest buildings, at the far end of the sandspit, date from the 18th century and host the **West Fjords Heritage Museum** (Byggðasafns Vestfjarða; Sudurtangi; www.nedsti.is; mid-May–mid-Sept daily 9am–6pm). Interesting exhibits and unusual nautical paraphernalia trace the development of Ísafjörður

Detour: Hólmavík to Krossneslaug

If it's true isolation you desire, it's worth making the five-hour round trip to Krossneslaug. Leaving Hólmavík on Route 61, after 10km (6 miles) Route 643 branches off to the north, over a causeway. Drangsnes, just east on Route 645, has three hotpots with ocean views. Route 643, impassable once autumn arrives, bumps its way to the old herring salting factory at Djúpavík, past tiny Gjögur airfield (the only way to access this area in winter), and on to Krossneslaug, a swimming pool at the edge of the world, before it gives up and peters out. The distance from Hólmavík to Krossneslaug is 107km (66 miles).

Hornstrandir is great walking country

and its fishing industry. In a tiny former shoe shop, **Skóbúðin – Museum of Everyday Life** (Hafnarstræti 5; www.facebook.com/museum.of.everyday.life/; June–Aug Wed–Sat noon–6pm) offers an unusually personal exhibition of local stories and memories.

West Tours (tel: 456 5111; www.west tours.is) is a co-operative of local tour

Hornstrandir peninsula

Hornstrandir has always been an inaccessible place, where winters came early, snow lasted longer and paths between the few habitations were hard. In the past, its few residents scratched a living from fishing, hunting birds and gathering eggs, but slowly drifted away elsewhere to easier lives, until by the 1950s, no one was left.

Now a protected nature reserve, Hornstrandir is a place of great beauty, with astonishing sandy bays and rugged cliffs. You can wade knee-deep in meadows of wild flowers, watch countless sea birds and listen at sundown for the bark of the Arctic fox. Traces of bridle paths crisscross the mountain passes, linking the fjords and inlets; there are no roads.

In summer, a ferry sails daily from Ísafjörður to Hornstrandir, bringing day-trippers, hikers and landowners who use the old farmsteads as summer cottages. See West Tours (Aðalstræti 7, Ísafjörður; tel: 456 5111; www.west-tours.is) for ferry schedules, tickets and walking tours that include tents and food. Independent visitors must be experienced hikers and take everything they need, as there is no tourist infrastructure.

Windmill, Vigur island

Arctic fox pups

operators and can arrange just about anything you might want to do, including **kayaking trips**; **whale watching** in the huge Ísafjarðardjúp fjord; and boat trips to two of the fjord's islands, **Vigur** and **Æðey** ('eider island'), with impressive

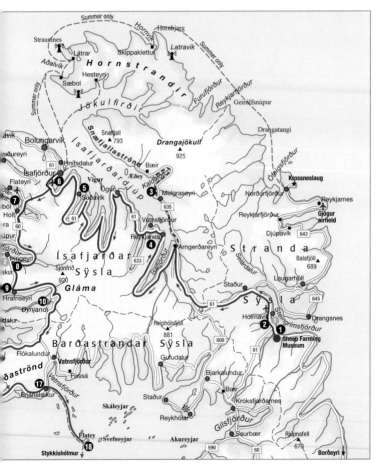

Hrafnseyri museum is dedicated to Jón Sigurðsson

birdlife, Iceland's only windmill and the smallest post office in Europe. They also run tours to the uninhabited nature reserve of **Hornstrandir** (see box).

ÍSAFJÖRÐUR TO PATREKSFJÖRÐUR

The drive from Ísafjörður to Patreksfjörður is spectacular, taking you over high mountain passes and alongside one of Iceland's most beautiful waterfalls. Each tiny fishing village along the way seems to have its own quirky museum.

Along Route 60

Driving west on Route 60 takes you through the Breiðadals/Botnsheiði tunnel, a single-lane 9km (5.5-mile) engineering masterpiece. One arm splits

---

Bolungarvík

About 12km (7 miles) north of Ísafjörður, Bolungarvík is an exposed spot, liable to landslides and avalanches. Ósvör Maritime Museum (www.osvor.is; June–mid-Aug Mon–Fri 9am–5pm, Sat–Sun 10am–5pm, mid-Aug–Sept Mon–Fri 11am–4pm) is in a restored fishing station and the Natural History Museum (Aðalstræti 21; www.nabo.is; same hours) has a jumble of stuffed animals including a seal and polar bear. Further west, the largely uninhabited coast is wild and imposing, with wind-lashed headlands and snow-capped peaks.

---

off northwest to **Suðureyri**, a village deprived of direct sunlight in winter for longer than anywhere else in Iceland.

The main road continues to **Önundarfjörður** ❼, with an unusual golden-sand beach: on rare sunny days, locals from nearby Flateyri bathe in the Greenland Sea. Cross Dýrafjörður to **Þingeyri** ❽, where there is a 'botanical garden', a little haven of carefully cultivated local plants. Stop for lunch at **Simbahöllin** (see ❷), before launching yourself up over the high mountain pass and down the breathtaking descent into **Hrafnseyri** ❾, the birthplace of Independence leader, Jón Sigurðsson, where a small **museum** (www.hrafnseyri.is; June–Aug daily 11am–6pm) is dedicated to his memory.

Twenty kilometres (12 miles) east, **Dynjandi waterfall** ❿, meaning 'the thundering one', is a spectacular collection of cascades quite rightly known as the jewel of the West Fjords.

West on Route 63

After the falls, branch off west on Route 63 to **Bildudalur** ⓫, which has an **Icelandic Sea Monster Museum** (Skrímslasetur; http://skrimsli.is; mid-May–mid-Sept daily 10am–6pm), with monstrous models of creatures said to lurk in the briny depths nearby. **Tálknafjörður** ⓬, 15km (9 miles) west, is a lively spot with a good swimming pool, bicycle hire and an adventure centre offering watersports and walking. Up the hillside are two open-air geothermal hotpots, **Pollurinn**, with

Café Riis, Hólmavík

beautiful views of the fjord. Continue to **Patreksfjörður** ⑬, with accommodation and dining options for the night.

LÁTRABJARG AND RAUÐASANDUR

After breakfast, set off to **Látrabjarg** ⑭, the most westerly point in Europe, for a bracing walk. What makes the long, pothole-filled journey along Route 612 so worthwhile is its sense of bleakness and the plunging **bird cliffs**. Thousands of puffins nest here in burrows. There are at least as many guillemots, plus the largest colony of razorbills in the world. Wrap up warm.

Retrace your steps along Route 612 to **Hnjótur** ⑮, home to the **Egill Ólafsson Museum** (Minjasafn Egils Ólafssonar; www.hnjotur.is; May–Sept daily 10am–6pm), with a dismantled plane outside. This is one man's lifetime accumulation of items, which give a glimpse of the resourceful nature of the West Fjords people. The museum café is good for coffee or a light lunch, depending on when you arrive.

Thirteen kilometres (8 miles) beyond the museum, turn right onto Route 614 – very steep, winding and gravelly – to reach the wonderful **beach** at **Rauðasandur** ⑯ The sand turns from red-orange to black, and superb surf thunders in from the Atlantic. There is a summer café. Depending on the tide, take a short hike to the ruins of **Sjöundaá farm**, where in 1802 an adulterous couple both murdered their partners so they could be together.

BRJÁNSLÆKUR FERRY

Head back to Route 612, then take Route 62 east, heading over the Kleyfarheiði mountain pass to **Brjánslækur** ⑰. From here, a ferry departs to Stykkishólmur (on the Snæfellsnes peninsula), calling in at the delightful island of **Flatey** ⑱ in summer. There are peaceful restored wooden houses; a fine little church, painted by Catalan artist Baltasar; and a nature reserve packed with divebombing Arctic terns.

Food and drink

❶ CAFÉ RIIS

Hafnarbraut 39, Hólmavík; tel: 451 3567; www.caferiis.is; daily 11.30am–9pm; $$
Hólmavík's popular café-bar has salad, pasta, fried chicken, burgers and pizzas, as well as the odd Icelandic dish – for example, *smjörsteiktar gellur* (fried cod tongues) – and a great seafood soup. Service is friendly and fast.

❷ SIMBAHÖLLIN

Fjarðargata 5, þingeyri; tel: 899 6659; www.simbahollin.is; daily mid-June–Aug 10am–10pm, mid-May–mid-June and early Sept noon–6pm; $$
Fabulous Simbahöllin ('Simbi's Palace') is the cosiest café, set in a beautifully renovated old Norwegian house from 1915. It does coffee, light lunches and renowned Belgian waffles, and serves as the village's cultural space, with live music and art exhibitions.

SNÆFELLSNES AND THE WEST

Snæfellsjökull icecap glints like a jewel in sunlight, set in a ring of rocky coves and traditional fishing villages, and surrounded by the wild Snæfellsnes peninsula, much of it a nature reserve. The more settled west is rich with historic saga sites.

DISTANCE: 315km (196 miles)
TIME: Three days
START: Stykkishólmur
END: Langjökull
POINTS TO NOTE: Walkers might want to allow an extra day for an ascent to the glacier or hikes in the nature reserve. Pack a swimsuit. Book ahead for a trip inside Langjökull (intotheglacier.is).

THE SNÆFELLSNES PENINSULA

Stykkishólmur

You could spend a happy half day in attractive **Stykkishólmur ❶**, full of brightly painted wooden houses, including the beautiful timber **Norwegian House** (Norska Húsið; www.norska-husid.is; June–Aug daily 11am–5pm), imported in kit form from Norway. The upper floor is decorated with period furniture and antiques, as it must have looked when William Morris stayed here in 1871.

Stykkishólmur's modern **church** overlooks the town. Also worth investigating is the **Library of Water** (Vatnasafn; https://www.facebook.com/vatnasafn; June–Aug daily 11am–5pm, Sept–May Tue–Sat 11am–5pm), formerly a library and now a contemplative installation by American artist Roni Horn.

The **Volcano Museum** (Eldfjallasafn; www.eldfjallasafn.is; May–Sept daily 11am–5pm; Oct–Apr Tue–Sat 11am–5pm) was set up by a local volcanologist to give visitors an insight into Iceland's explosive character.

Daily summer **boat tours** (www.seatours.is) sail around some of Breiðafjörður's 2,700 tiny islands from the pretty little harbour, catching crabs, scallops, starfish and whelk for passengers to snack on. A car/passenger ferry sails to the West Fjords, calling in at **Flatey island** (see page 97) in summer.

Stop for lunch at **Sjávarpakkhúsið** (see ❶) before leaving town. On the way out, 2km (1.2 miles) past the airfield is a short turnoff to **Helgafell ❷** ('Holy Hill'), site of an ancient temple to Thor, and

Solitary house, Snæfellsjökull National Park

home of Guðrún Ósvífursdóttir, the main protagonist of *Laxdæla Saga*. Climbing it in silence without looking back is said to grant you three wishes.

To the end of the peninsula

Following Route 54 west, 20km (12 miles) outside Stykkishólmur is the turnoff (signposted 'Helgafellssveit') to the farm **Bjarnarhöfn** ❸ (www.bjarnarhofn.is; daily June–Aug 9am–8pm, Sept–May 9am–6pm), with an exhibition about shark fishing, and an opportunity to taste fermented shark produced in the curing shed.

Continuing on Route 54 brings you to the small fishing village of **Grundarfjörður** ❹. Its beautifully symmetrical mountain **Kirkjufell** ❺ is the most-photographed in Iceland – even more so since it starred as 'mountain shaped like an arrowhead' in *Game of Thrones*. From November to April, killer whales follow the herring into the fjord here: **Láki Tours** (tel: 546 6808; www.lakitours.com) sail out to meet them.

In summer, the same company runs whale-watching trips from **Ólafsvík** ❻, a further 25km (15.5 miles) west – turn off onto Route 574, which runs around the tip of the peninsula. Just beyond, the area between the tiny settlements of **Rif** ❼ and **Hellissandur** ❽ is rich with birdlife, and has one of the largest Arctic tern nesting areas in Europe – you have been warned. The Arctic tern is the symbol of Snæfellsbær, spending winter in the Antarctic, then migrating north for summer – flying a distance of up to 40,000km (25,000 miles) per year. You'll find simple accommodation in the area if you want to break the route here.

Snæfellsjökull National Park

Hellissandur marks the start of **Snæfellsjökull National Park**, an area of great beauty, bounded by the sea. At its heart is enigmatic **Snæfellsjökull** ❾, 1,445 metres (4,740ft) high and permanently snow-capped. The glacier was made famous by Jules Verne as the entry point for his *Journey to the Centre of the Earth* and also plays a role in *Under the Glacier,* by Nobel Prize-winning Icelandic novelist Halldór Laxness.

If you want to get up onto the glacier, from May to August, you can go by bus/snowmobile with www.theglacier.is – allow three hours; or Summit Adventure Guides (www.summitguides.is) can take you on day hikes with crampons and snowshoes year-round.

Summit also runs 45-minute tours to **Vatnshellir cave** ❿ (mid-May–Sept 10am–6pm), an amazing 8,000-year-old lava tube, which set off on the hour from a small car park 1.2km (0.75 miles) before the turn-off to Malariff.

The **national park visitor centre** (summer daily 10am–5pm, winter Mon–Fri 11am–4pm) at **Malariff** ⓫, near the lighthouse, sells maps of interesting walking trails in the area.

Arched rock formation, Arnarstapi

South coast

The seaside and cliffs between **Hellnar** ⑫ and **Arnarstapi** ⑬ are a nature reserve, packed with birdlife and fascinating basalt formations, ravines and grottoes. A 2.5km (1.5 miles) hiking trail leads through the lava fields between the two tiny settlements, with **Fjöruhúsið café** (see ②) to fortify you for the walk, and overnight accommodation at both places.

Bárður Snæfellsás – half man, half troll – was one of the original Norwegian settlers in this region. After a family dispute, Bárður pushed both his nephews off a cliff, gave away all his possessions and disappeared into the glacier. Since then, his spirit is said to protect the area, and is called on in times of need. Many places are named after him – for example, **Bárðarlaug** ('Bárður's Pool'), a small and peaceful lake a 10-minute walk from Hellnar – and a huge **statue** of him by sculptor Ragnar Kjartansson guards Arnarstapi.

After overnighting in Hellnar or Arnarstapi, continue your journey along the south coast, rejoining Route 54 near Búðir. Four hundred metres (440ft) further is **Bjarnarfoss** ⑭ waterfall (on private property, so admire it from a distance): some people see a *fjallkona* (Lady of the Mountain) inside the falls, with a veil of water droplets falling around her shoulders.

Fjöruhúsið café   *Fairytale Hraunfossar waterfall*

Stop for a quick morning dip at **Lýsuhólslaug** ⑮ (June–mid-Aug daily 11am–8.30pm), 2km (1.2 miles) off Route 54, a green pool with naturally fizzy water. You can drink the same stuff straight from the source at the farm **Ölkelda** ⑯ ('ale spring'); the rusty-tasting water is fabled to have healing properties.

Roughly 30km (19 miles) east, just past the turn-off to Route 567, an unnumbered dirt road heads a few kilometres north to **Gerðuberg** ⑰. This natural formation looks almost manmade, with evenly spaced 10-metre (33ft) -high basalt columns stretching out in a long wall along the cliff face.

Head for a late lunch in Borgarnes, 30km (19 miles) south on Route 54.

BORGARNES
AND AROUND

Borgarnes ⑱, near the mouth of the Borgarfjörður, is essentially a service centre for the neighbouring dairy farms, but it's worth stopping for lunch at **Búðarklettur** (see ③), the café of the **Settlement Centre of Iceland** (www.landnam.is; daily 10am–9pm). After you've eaten, investigate the centre's two fascinating exhibitions. One explores the settlement of Iceland, and the other uses striking sound and visuals to tell the tale of Egill Skallagrímsson, the intriguing hero of *Egils Saga*, and his bloodthirsty deeds. The town also contains the **burial mound**

of Egill's father, who claimed land here during the settlement.

Cross the stunning causeway south of town, then turn east onto Route 50. Turn left on Route 511 to **Hvanneyri** ⑲ for artisanal Icelandic-made sweaters – **Ullarselið** (http://ull.is; June–Aug daily 11am–5pm, Sept–May Thu–Sat 1–5pm) combs, spins and knits its sheep's wool by hand.

REYKHOLT AND AROUND

If sweaters aren't you're thing, continue on Route 50 to the junction with Route 518. On the left just beyond the junction is **Deildartunguhver** ⑳, Europe's most powerful hot spring, which pumps out 180 litres (40 gallons) of boiling water per second. A chic spa/restaurant, **Krauma** (daily June–Aug 10am–11pm, Sept–May 10am–9pm), opened here at the end of 2017, with five hot baths fed by the spring.

Reykholt
For another important saga pilgrimage site, turn onto Route 518. **Reykholt** ㉑ was once home to Snorri Sturluson (1179–1241), politician extraordinaire and immortal saga-writer, who was murdered here after falling foul of the Norwegian king. You can visit **Snorralaug**, the bathing pool where the chieftain would receive visitors and, beside it, the partly restored remains of a tunnel that led to his farmhouse. **Snorrast-**

ofa (www.snorrastofa.is; Apr–Sept daily 10am–6pm, Oct–Apr Mon–Fri 10am–5pm), located just next to the church, is a research centre dedicated to Snorri, and contains an exhibition about his life and work.

Húsafell

At **Húsafell** ㉒, 25km (15.5 miles) to the east on Route 518, many Icelanders have holiday cottages from which they explore the surrounding area. Just before the village is magnificent **Hraunfossar**, a multitude of tiny cascades that materialise out of the lava, and **Barnafoss**, which tumbles into the Hvíta River nearby.

The landscape is riddled with **caves**, hidden inside the 52km (32-mile) -long Hallmundarhraun lava flow. Get to the farm Fljótstunga, 14km (9 miles) beyond Húsafell on Route 518 and then the farm road, in time for the last tour of **Víðgelmir cave** ㉓ (tel: 783 3600; www.thecave.is; June–Aug on the hour 9am–6pm, less frequently rest of year), with a walkway leading underground into the multicoloured lava.

Langjökull glacier

Iceland's second largest glacier, **Langjökull** ㉔, is nearby. If you want to visit the man-made **labyrinth of tunnels** (https://intotheglacier.is) that have been drilled into the icecap, you'll want to spend the night in Húsafell (transfer bus from Húsafell to Klaki 9.20am June–mid-Oct, 10am mid-Oct–May).

Food and drink

① SJÁVARPAKKHÚSIÐ

Hafnargata 2, 340 Stykkishólmur; tel: 438 1800; www.sjavarpakkhusid.is; daily noon–10pm; $$$

This seafood restaurant down by the harbour has one vegan dish, but then it's seafood all the way. The menu changes daily, according to what the fishing boats outside the window have brought in that morning.

② FJÖRUHÚSIÐ CAFÉ

Hellnar; tel: 435 6844; daily May–mid-June and Sept–mid-Nov noon–6pm, mid-June–Aug 10am–9pm; $$

Fjöruhúsið is a sweet little seaside café offering home-made food, including fresh bread, cakes and waffles, and savoury seafood soup. Inside its white-painted walls bounce the light around; in good weather sit on the terrace and look for whales.

③ BÚÐARKLETTUR

Brákarbraut 13–15, Borgarnes; tel: 437 1600; www.landnam.is; daily 11.30am–3pm; $$$

The Settlement Centre's restaurant serves hearty pasta, fish and meat mains. Many have a traditional slant – think smoked lamb and herring on rye bread – and there's a larger vegetarian selection than in most Icelandic restaurants.

Brave campers along the Kjölur route

THE INTERIOR: KJÖLUR ROUTE

Home to Iceland's wildest, most extreme scenery, the vast, empty interior can only be accessed by 4WD or mountain vehicles at the very height of summer. The Kjölur route follows an ancient byway used in saga times.

DISTANCE: 200km (125 miles)
TIME: One to three days, depending on how you choose to break the journey
START: Gullfoss
END: Blönduós
POINTS TO NOTE: You might want to combine this trip with the Sprengisandur route (see page 107), as both take in highlights of the lonely interior region. Build in time to rest at the start and end of the route; hikers can make use of the mountain huts along the way. Remember to bring swimsuits and walking gear.

Iceland's huge, barren interior has never been inhabited: only medieval outlaws, banished from civilised villages on the fertile coast, have ever haunted this desolate region. The hostile highlands were not for living in, but were a place to cross as quickly as possible if one had to travel from north to south.

Today the interior is still a bleak region, which can only be accessed by vehicles – 4WD jeeps or high-suspension mountain buses – at the very height of summer once the snow has melted. Normal hire cars cannot ford the rivers or cope with the pitted, rubble-strewn F-roads, and are certainly not covered by insurance. The easiest and cheapest way to get to the highlands is by mountain bus, either on scheduled services or through private tour operators.

Scheduled buses cover the two main north–south routes, Kjölur (F35, also known as the Kjalvegur; bus service 610/610a) and Sprengisandur (see page107; F26; bus service 14/14a). With the Highland Circle Passport (ISK49,300) from Reykjavík Excursions (www.re.is), you can travel in a circle on the Kjölur and Sprengisandur highland routes, either clockwise or anti-clockwise.

The Kjölur route is the most popular crossing through the central highlands. The schedule bus 610/610a (late June–early Sept daily) from Reykjavík also calls at Hveragerði, Selfoss and Laugarvatn on the way to Gull-

Boiling pools splash mineral–rich waters across the rocks to colour the mountains of Kerlingarfjöll

foss. Based on an ancient byway used in saga times, the Kjölur route then extends from Gullfoss to the Blöndudalur, passing between the Langjökull and Hofsjökull ice-caps. Bus services continue on to Akureyri.

The only forms of accommodation are camping or a few mountain huts, mostly operated by Ferðafélag Íslands (Iceland Touring Association; tel: 568 2533; www.fi.is). The huts are in extremely high demand, so you will need to plan carefully and book well in advance if you want to get off the buses and go hiking.

Hvítá river

The weather is generally very unpredictable – even in high summer, snowfalls and blizzards can occur – so always be prepared for the worst.

INTO THE WILD

Leaving **Gullfoss** ❶ (see page 53), the grassland on the plain above the falls soon changes to lichen-dotted stones. There is a steady drop in temperature as the landscape becomes increasingly bleak and uninviting.

On the skyline the only relief is the snow-sprinkled mass of **Mount Bláfell** ❷ (1,204 metres/3,950ft). Skirting around the bulk of Mount Bláfell to the east, the track descends to the **River Hvítá**, crossing four or five tributary streams and small rivers. A spectacular view opens up across desolate dark tundra towards the large glacial lake **Hvítárvatn** ❸, created by the distant blue glaciers of **Langjökull** icecap. On the horizon lies another icecap, **Hofsjökull**; conflicting winds from the two create swirling dust clouds in between. From the bridge over the Hvítá, there is a clear view to the lake. Small icebergs can usually be seen in the water, and on the far shore towers the outlet glacier from which they originated.

Hikers might want to jump off at the **Árbúðir hut** ❹ (tel: 486 8757, 895 9500 or 867 3571; http://gljasteinn. is), directly on the route, for a more extended exploration of the area.

Don't attempt the route without a 4WD jeep

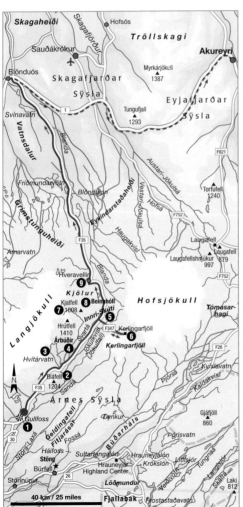

INNRI-SKÚTI

Beyond, the brown dusty plain turns to gravel and then a great black stretch of volcanic clinker, with mountains and glaciers always on the horizon. The track crosses the southern stony slopes of the small mountain **Innri-Skúti ⑤**. As well as affording a panoramic view over the **Jökulfall** river valley to the Hofsjökull icecap and Kerlingarfjöll mountains, the slopes are particularly rich in tundra plants. Most are no more than tiny specks that eke out an existence sheltered between the rocks. Small pink cushions of moss campion compete with white mountain avens and other alpines for space. Dwarf willows grow barely centimetres above the ground, crushed by the constant wind.

THE KERLINGARFJÖLL REGION

The bus takes a detour down track F347 to drop

Relaxing in a natural hot spring

off and collect passengers from **Kerlingarfjöll 6** (tel: 664 7000 or 664 7878; www.kerlingarfjoll.is), one of the few places in the highlands that is open all year – in winter, access is by Super Jeep or snowmobile. Facilities here are uncommonly good for the highlands, with made-up beds, sleeping-bag accommodation, a campsite, café-restaurant, electricity, a mobile-phone signal and hot tubs.

The wider Kerlingarfjöll region is an excellent climbing area with superb views of Hofsjökull, deep ravines and well-vegetated slopes. The bleak mountain peaks, rising to 1,400 metres (4,600ft), are made of rhyolite, making a stark contrast to the dark plains of Kjölur. In a succession of small gorges, sulphur and boiling water vent to the surface, and the rocks are splashed green, red and yellow by the mineral-laden waters.

KJALFELL AND BEINAHÓLL

When the bus returns to the main Kjölur route, you will see the table-mountain **Kjalfell 7** (1,008 metres/3,307ft). To the northeast, on a low lava ridge, is **Beinahóll 8** ('hill of bones'). In

1780, four men from Reynistaður farm in Skagafjörður perished here in bad weather with a flock of sheep. Because of this incident, most travellers over Kjölur for the next hundred years chose to pass on the west of Kjalfell, instead of using the main track to the east of the mountain.

HVERAVELLIR AND BEYOND

Hveravellir 9 (www.hveravellir. is), 100km (60 miles) from Gullfoss, is a hot-spring oasis within the cold desert. Deep pools of brilliant, near-boiling blue water are lined with white silica; all around are small mud pools of black, brown and red minerals. The bus stops for an hour at Hveravellir so people can look around or enjoy a bathe. However, you might want to stay longer at this comfortable highland hub, with two touring huts, a campsite, summer café, small shop and petrol station. Other sights in the area include the hot springs Bláhver; roaring, screaming Öskurshólshver; and Eyvindarhver, named after the 18th-century outlaw Fjalla-Eyvindur. Ruins of the outlaw's shelter, where he lived with his baby-smothering wife Halla Jónsdóttir, can be found nearby on the edge of the lava.

From Hveravellir, a rough track runs north, meeting up with the hard road at the **Blöndudalur**, 110km (68 miles) away, before continuing via **Blönduós** and **Varmahlíð** to **Akureyri**.

Food and drink

As you'd expect, the interior lacks even simple, stand-alone restaurants. Bring supplies with you and take advantage of facilities in Kerlingaftjöll and Hveravellir.

The mighty Goðafoss waterfall

THE INTERIOR: SPRENGISANDUR ROUTE

This tour takes in areas of Iceland's interior so desolate that Apollo astronauts prepared here for their moon landings. One of two main routes to traverse the interior, the Sprengisandur extends to the beautiful and remote area around Lanmannalaugar.

DISTANCE: 225km (140 miles)
TIME: One to three days, depending on how you choose to break the journey
START: Goðafoss
END: Landmannalaugar
POINTS TO NOTE: You might want to combine this trip with the Kjölur route (see page 103), which also explores the interior region – if so, look into the Highland Circle Passport (ISK49,300; https://www.re.is/iceland-on-your-own/passports/highland-circle-passport/). Long-distance bus tours can be grisly, bum-numbing experiences, so try to break up the journey. Bring a swimsuit for the hot pools.

During the Age of Settlement, few Viking colonists braved the desolation of the interior. By the 13th century, however, some paths had been created through the Central Highlands as short cuts to reduce the journey time when travelling from north to south. Today, 800 years later, the vast region of the interior is still almost totally uninhabited.

This large, empty region is Iceland's premier attraction for adventurous travellers. But accessibility is tough – roads are reduced to mere tracks, passable only to 4WD jeeps or high-suspension mountain buses in the middle of summer. The weather is unpredictable and camping is the main form of accommodation, although there are a few huts, which hikers may want to take advantage of (see page 103), plus the Hrauneyjar motel (www.hrauneyjar.is) and Kiðagil guesthouse (www.kidagil.is) at either end of the Sprengisandur route.

The Sprengisandur route (F26) runs from the Bárðardalur between Akureyri and Lake Mývatn to Þjórsá, east of Selfoss; it covers some of the most desolate ground in the country. Scheduled bus service 17/17a runs directly between Mývatn and Reykjavík via Sprengisandur; but this bus bypasses Landmannalaugar. Instead, take scheduled bus service 14/14a, which leaves the N1 petrol station at Mývatn at 8am (July and August, Monday, Wednesday, Friday) and goes to Landmannalaugar. If you'd rather, book onto a private tour.

It is possible to swim in Víti crater

WATERFALL COUNTRY

The bus travels west from Mývatn on Route 1 to the start of the route at **Goðafoss ❶**, where it stops for 45 minutes for passengers to marvel at the falls. After that, it lurches south onto Route 842 then F26 through the Bárðardalur. A scraped road soon degrades into a rough track, which climbs past the beautiful waterfall of **Aldeyjarfoss ❷** with its tall basalt columns, where the bus stops for half an hour. On clear days there are spectacular views across the Ódáðahraun lava plain towards Askja (see box). The shield volcano of Trölladyngja is clear on the horizon to the south.

THE INTERIOR PROPER

The bus bounces along beside the braided Skjálfandafljót river for many a mile. In the middle of nowhere, the track forks, with the F881 running off west to **Laugafell ❸**, with a mountain hut and several warm springs. According to an old tale, a woman named Þórunn, daughter of Iceland's last Catholic bishop, brought her family to stay here in the 15th century to escape the Black Death. Laugafell is only accessible by private 4WD or by walking.

Then the gravel expanse of the Sprengisandur truly begins, with magnificent vistas eastwards to **Vatnajökull** and the smaller icecap of **Tungnafellsjökull** and westwards to **Hofsjökull**. A number of river crossings later, the blue tongues of glaciers come into view. At **Nýidalur ❹**,

Fjallabak Nature Reserve   *Herðubreið*

close to the geographical centre of Iceland, stand several huts – invariably a welcome sight. There is a small campsite on the only patch of green in the area, but even in the middle of summer high winds and near-freezing temperatures make it a desperate option.

Askja and Herðubreið

From Mývatn, another full-day bus tour (www.visitaskja.com; 12 hours; late June–early Sept) takes in the Askja caldera and the nature reserve Herðubreiðarlindir. The bus leaves at 7.45am daily from the supermarket in Reykjahlíð. Highlights include:

Ódáðahraun plateau. The moonlike landscape where US astronauts Neil Armstrong and Buzz Aldrin came to train for their 1969 moon landing. This intimidating flat expanse is the world's largest lava flow, stretching almost to the horizon.

Herðubreiðarlindir. A wonderful oasis in the middle of the black sands and lava, rich in birdlife, vegetation and water springs. Herðubreið, 1,682 metres (5,518ft) high, is known as the queen of Iceland's mountains.

Askja caldera. Forty-five sq km (16 sq mile) of black lava, cream pumice screes and white snow. This was the scene of epic eruptions in 1874–5 when vents under lake Öskjuvatn threw out two billion cubic metres of ash. On the edge of the lake, the crater Víti ('Hell') contains milky-blue water that is still warm from the last eruption in 1961 – bring a swimsuit.

The dusty track south crosses the mountain of **Kistualda** (790 metres/2,600ft), with panoramic views, before continuing to **Þórisvatn** ❺ (Iceland's second largest lake) through a landscape of glaciers and black gravel plains. Just beyond the lake and on the main track is a veritable metropolis in this desolation: the **Hrauneyjar Highland Center** ❻ (www.hrauneyjar. is) at Hrauneyjafoss, with a petrol station, a café-restaurant and a guesthouse.

LANDMANNALAUGAR

The bus makes a 15-minute stop for passengers to stretch their legs, before continuing for the last hour to **Landmannalaugar** ❼, where it terminates. Landmannalaugar's spectacular rhyolitic hills are bright yellow, green and red, dotted with deep blue lakes. There are hot springs here, and steam rises from every corner of the valley. The hut and camping facilities make a good base for fabulous walks in the Fjallabak Nature Reserve.

From Landmannalaugar, you can take bus 11/11a west to Reykjavík (mid-June to mid-September five daily); or bus 10/10a east to Skaftafell (mid-June to August daily at 3.30pm), which stops for an hour at **Eldgjá canyon** on the way.

Food and drink

Options are sparse – ensure you have your own supplies and tuck into what's on offer at the Hrauneyjar Highland Centre.

ÖKULSÁRLÓN **GULLFOSS** **EYJAFJA**

ÖKULL MÝVATN HORNSTRANDIR

DIRECTORY

Hand-picked hotels and restaurants to suit all budgets and tastes, organised by area, plus select nightlife listings, an alphabetical listing of practical information, a language guide and an overview of the best books and films to give you a flavour of the country.

Enjoying dinner at Hótel Holt

ACCOMMODATION

The range of hotel and guesthouse accommodation in Iceland is wide. In Reykjavík there are some very stylish, world-class hotels – with prices to match. Elsewhere in the country, farms and guesthouses are the norm, and the few hotels tend to lack character, although stunning locations often compensate. Thin walls and curtains are common – light sleepers should bring earplugs and an eye mask.

Iceland's three hotel chains are Icelandair Hotels (tel: 444 4000, www.icelandairhotels.com), with eight hotels around the country; Fosshótel (tel: 562 4000, www.fosshotel.is), with 14 hotels; and Keahotels (www.keahotels.is), with eight hotels in Reykjavík, Akureyri and Mývatn. Their best deals are online.

Icelandair-owned Hotel Edda (tel: 444 4000; www.hoteledda.is) opens 10 of Iceland's schools, universities and conference centres as summer-only hotels, which can be an economical option.

There are guesthouses everywhere in Iceland, and these are generally clean and welcoming. Bathrooms are usually shared. Lots of farms offer guesthouse accommodation – Hey Iceland (tel: 570 2700, www.heyiceland.is) is a farmer-owned travel agency with over 170 farmhouses on its books.

HI Iceland (www.hostel.is) runs 34 great youth hostels, many with private rooms that are of the same standard as a typical guesthouse.

The free brochure *Áning*, available from tourist offices, lists hotels, guesthouses, summer houses, hostels and campsites countrywide. Inspired by Iceland (www.inspiredbyiceland.com) has accommodation lists, searchable by type and location.

Early online bookings are recommended for high season (mid-May to mid-September), when prices often double and rooms can be hard to come by. Outside these months, some hotels and guesthouses close for winter.

Price guidelines below are for a double room with bathroom in high season, including breakfast and tax, unless otherwise stated. Hotels usually accept payment by credit card, but payment for guesthouses, farms, hostels and campsites is generally cash-only.

$$$$ = over ISK30,000
$$$ = SK24,000–30,000
$$ = ISK15,000–24,000
$ = below ISK15,000

Reykjavík

Arcturus Guesthouse
Sólvallagata 20; tel: 770 4629; www.hotelborg.is/, www.arcturus.is; $$
Named after the brightest star in the northern sky, Arcturus is one of Reykjavík's newest guesthouses, a smidgen

Hótel Borg, an Icelandic institution

to the west of the city centre in a quiet residential district. Its plain but pleasant rooms all have shared bathrooms.

Eyja Guldsmeden

Brautarholt 10; tel: 519 7300; www.hotelborg.is/, www.hoteleyja.is; $$$$

Any faint concerns about the unglamorous street dissolve upon entering this cosy boutique hotel, a 10-minute walk from the heart of town. All rooms contain simple wooden four-poster beds, softened with fluffy bedspreads, and bathroom products are all eco-friendly.

Guesthouse Sunna

Þórsgata 26; tel: 511 5570; www.hotelborg.is, https://sunna.is; $$

Sunna offers a choice of simple, bright, clean rooms with private or shared bathrooms, and one- and two-bedroom apartments, many with views of Hallgrimskirkja. There are fridges and kettles in the shared kitchenettes on every floor.

Hótel Borg

Pósthússtræti 11; tel: 551 1440; www.hotelborg.is; $$$$

This imposing building near the Icelandic Parliament is a national institution. Rooms are beautifully renovated in modern style, with nods to its Art Deco heritage. The restaurant is a Jamie Oliver Italian.

Hótel Holt

Bergstaðastræti 37; tel: 552 5700; www.holt.is; $$$$

A long-standing luxury hotel, famous for its superb restaurant and artworks, which form the largest private collection of Icelandic paintings in existence. Decor is very traditional – think leather, dark woodwork and quiet lounge areas.

Hótel Leifur Eríksson

Skólavörðustígur 45; tel: 562 0800; www.hotelleifur.is; $$$

A friendly family-run place with a prime location right opposite Hallgrímskirkja church. Rooms are basic but comfortable. There is no restaurant, although a continental breakfast is included and hot drinks are available 24 hours a day.

Icelandair Hotel Reykjavík Marina

Mýrargata 2; tel: 444 4000, 560 8000; www.icelandairhotels.com; $$$$

This Icelandair hotel has a laidback ambience, quirky contemporary decor and harbour views. It's worth splashing out for one of the larger deluxe rooms. The hotel bar Slippbarinn is a celebrated nightspot, with live music and weekend DJs.

Loft Hostel

Bankastræti 7; tel: 553 8140; www.lofthostel.is; $$

Loft is the newest of three HI Iceland hostels in Reykjavík, with sunny staff, a café-bar and rooftop deck with fabulous city views, and free events like painting nights, pub quizzes and Sunday yoga. Dorm beds and private rooms available.

Pretty Hótel Framtíð

Óðinsvé

Oðinstorg 11; tel: 511 6200;
www.hotelodinsve.is; $$$$

A relaxed atmosphere and excellent staff make this hotel, in a quiet residential quarter close to the centre, a comfortable place to stay. Standard rooms are a little spartan, but the apartment-like split-level deluxe rooms are very nice indeed.

Reykjavik Residence Hotel

Hverfisgata 45; tel: 561 1200;
www.hotelborg.is/www.rrhotel.is; $$$$

For beauty, elegance and a high level of service, look no further than the Reykjavik Residence Hotel. The apartments, scattered across three historic buildings, range from small studios to the suites where King Christian X and Queen Alexandrina of Denmark stayed in 1926.

Room with a View

Laugavegur 18; tel: 552 7262;
www.roomwithaview.is; $$$$

For a good, cost-effective alternative to a hotel, try these comfortable serviced apartments on the main shopping street. The 44 options range from small basement studios to a 12-bed beast – check the website for further details.

Storm Hótel

Þórunnartún 4; tel: 518 3000;
www.hotelborg.is/www.keahotels.is; $$$

A new, stylish, modern place, with lots of glass, polished hardwood floors, cool colours and soothing photographs of Iceland's scenery. Located in Reykjavík's business district, a 15-minute walk from the city centre.

Three Sisters Guesthouse

Ránargata 16; tel: 565 2181;
www.threesisters.is; $$$

A splendid alternative to a hotel room, these cosy studio apartments, in a peaceful old house, come with small kitchenettes. The area, near the harbour, is very quiet, yet just a few strides away from the city-centre action.

Reykjanes

Northern Lights Inn

Norðurljósavegur 1, Grindavík; tel: 426 8650; www.nli.is; $$$$

In the middle of a lava field, a 15-minute walk from the Blue Lagoon, this inn has 42 quiet and spacious rooms and a fabulous on-site restaurant. In winter, if requested, staff will wake you up if the northern lights appear.

The Southwest

Frost and Fire Hotel

Hverhamar, Hveragerði; tel: 483 4959;
www.frostogfuni.is; $$$$

Tucked into a ravine, Frost and Fire has cosy, chalet-like rooms, where the sound of the nearby river lulls you to sleep. There are hot tubs, a pool and a small spa, as well as an excellent restaurant.

Hotel Edda IKI Laugarvatn & ML Laugarvatn

Laugarvatn; tel: 444 4000; www.hoteledda.is; $$

There are not one but two Edda hotels in this popular holiday town, open early June to mid/late August. IKI is the nicer of the two, with just 28 rooms, all with private bathrooms, and half with lake views.

Icelandair Hotel Vik

Klettsvegur 1–5, Vík; tel: 444 4000, 487 1480; www.icelandairhotels.com; $$$$

The new wing of this Icelandair hotel is where you want to stay – the clean, modern, Scandinavian-style rooms are good sized, with floor-to-ceiling windows that let in the sea light. In winter, a northern lights wake-up call is available.

Stracta Hotel

Rangárflatir 4, Hella; tel: 531 8010; www.stractahotels.is; $$$

This family-run hotel, in the centre of Hella, has rooms decorated in typical Nordic style, with neutral colours and parquet floors. Cheaper rooms have shared bathrooms. There are two saunas and hot tubs in the courtyard.

The Southeast

Hali Country Hotel

Hali, 781 Hornafjörður; tel: 478 1073; http://hali.is; $$$$

Once the farm of writer Þórbergur Þórðarson, this lovely seaside spot near Jökulsárlón glacial lagoon has 18 clean, quiet rooms and an excellent restaurant, serving char from the pool over the road.

Icelandair Hotel Klaustur

Klausturvegur 6, Kirkjubæjarklaustur; tel: 444 4000, 487 4900; www.icelandairhotels. com; $$$

Hotel Klaustur is the only hotel in this one-street 'town'. Rooms are on the austere side, but are clean, quiet and comfortable. The above-average restaurant makes use of local ingredients, such as Arctic char caught in Systravatn lake.

Milk Factory

Dalbraut 2, Höfn; tel: 478 8900; http://milkfactory.is; $$

Seventeen rooms, stylishly renovated in 2016 and done out in soothing greys, make up this friendly guesthouse on the very edge of Höfn, in an old milk factory. The spacious family rooms have two storeys.

Heimaey

Hótel Vestmannaeyjar

Vestmannabraut 28; tel: 481 2900; www. hotelvestmannaeyjar.is; $$$

In this comfortable small-town hotel, you're made to feel like an old friend as soon as you step through the door. The hotel is also the reception for the HI hostel Sunnuhóll ($), round the back.

The East Fjords

Hótel Framtíð

Vogaland 4, 765 Djúpivogur; tel: 478 8887; www.hotelframtid.is; $$$

Djúpivogur's only hotel, in an old building by the harbour, has rustic pine-panelled rooms with/without bathroom, as well as apartments, chalet-style holiday cottages and a campsite down the

Hôtel Ti[1884]

road. Try to get a room with a view of the water.

Lake Hotel Egilsstadir

Egilsstaðir; tel: 471 1114;
http://english.lakehotel.is; $$$

This stone farmhouse recreates the atmosphere of early 20th-century rural Iceland in its 1903 building, with romantic decor and period antiques, while rooms in the new building are furnished in contemporary style. Facilities include a spa and up-market restaurant.

Óbyggðasetur Íslands – Wilderness Center

Egilsstadir 701; tel: 440 8822, 896 2339;
www.wilderness.is; $$

At the end of remote Norðurdalur, unwind with home-cooked food, beautiful waterfalls walks, horse riding, fishing, a museum... and no TVs! Wood-panelled double, single and dorm rooms ($) conjure up a sense of times gone by.

The Northeast

Hótel Norðurljós

Aðalbraut 2, Raufarhöfn; tel: 465 1233;
http://hotelnordurljos.is; $$

This externally rather unattractive building once housed the herring girls, who came to salt fish during Raufarhöfn's boom-years. It's been a hotel for over 40 years, welcoming visitors with basic but clean rooms and a good bar-restaurant with sea views.

Kaldbaks Kot

Kaldbakur, Húsavík; tel: 892 1744;
www.cottages.is; $$

These snug log cabins, overlooking the sea one mile from Húsavík, make the perfect base for self-caterers: they have large terraces, and contain all the facilities you need, plus there are hot pots from which you can enjoy the idyllic surroundings.

Mývatn

Hotel Laxá

Olnbogaás, 660 Mývatn; tel: 464 1900;
www.hotellaxa.is; $$$

On the south shore of the lake, just west of Skútustaðir, this newly built hotel has 360° views of lava plains and the lake, with no other habitations in sight. Spacious rooms have sleek Scandinavian decor, and bathrooms have power showers.

Hótel Reynihlíð

Reykjahlíð; tel: 464 4170;
www.myvatnhotel.is; $$$$

Accommodation at Mývatn is limited and expensive. This long-standing hotel is one of the best options: newer rooms are smart and modern, and there is a lively café-bar in the old farm next door.

Akureyri & Around

ÁS Guesthouse

Eyrarlandsvegur 33, Akureyri; tel: 863 3247;
http://asguesthouse.is; $$

Akureyri has some great family-run guesthouses, including ÁS, situated in a charming location next to the botanic

garden and with stunning fjord views. There are four spacious, sunny rooms (three with balconies), which have been immaculately refitted.

Hótel Kea

Hafnarstræti 87–9, Akureyri; tel: 460 2000; www.hotelkea.is; $$$$

A reliable and comfortable hotel, the Kea is close to restaurants and shops. The rooms have mini-bars and satellite television. Keahotels also owns cheaper Hótel Norðurland ($$$), next door.

The Northwest

Hótel Arctic Tindastóll

Lindargata 3, Sauðárkrókur; tel: 453 5002; www.arctichotels.is; $$$

Built in 1884, Hótel Tindastóll is the oldest hotel in Iceland and one of the most unusual. Its ample rooms, with timber beams and traditional charm, come with all modern amenities. Marlene Dietrich stayed here during World War II.

The West Fjords

Fosshótel Westfjords

Patreksfjörður; tel: 456 2004; www.fosshotel.is; closed Nov–Feb; $$$

Patreksfjörður has one hotel, the perfectly decent three-star Fosshótel. Most of its 40 clean, comfortable rooms have views of either the fjord or the mountains, and there is a good restaurant.

Hotel Flatey

Flatey Island, Breiðafjörður; tel: 555 7788; open June–Aug; $$

This summer hotel on Flatey island offers just 11 simple but romantic wood-panelled rooms, decorated in Scandinavian style with fresh flowers; all have shared bathrooms. Excellent fresh fish and Breiðafjörður blue mussels are served at its restaurant with home-baked bread.

Hótel Ísafjörður

Silfurtorg 2, Ísafjörður; tel: 456 4111; www.hotelisafjordur.is; $$$

Standard rooms at this hotel, right in the town centre, are average: it's worth paying extra for deluxe. The highlight is the good restaurant with its fine fjord views.

Snæfellsnes and the West

Fosshótel Hellnar

Brekkubær, 356 Hellnar; tel: 435 6820; www.fosshotel.is; $$$

One of Fosshótel's best properties, Hellnar is in a spectacular setting, with sea and mountain views. The hotel is decorated in cool neutrals that accentuate the northern light. Some rooms are a little small, but all are very clean and comfortable.

Hotel Husafell

Húsafell 311, Borgarbyggð; tel: 435 1551; http://hotelhusafell.com; $$$

The only hotel in Húsafell is – fortunately – this extremely cosy, tasteful option. Rooms have warm wooden floors, large windows to take in the scenery, and paintings by local artist Páll Guðmundsson. It has a geothermal pool and an excellent restaurant.

RESTAURANTS

Over the last 10 years, Iceland has been greatly inspired by the 'New Nordic Kitchen' movement, which has had a revolutionary effect on northern cuisine. The country's chefs take great pride in using Iceland's natural larder – fish, lamb, goose, reindeer, seaweed, moss, rhubarb – to reinvent and revitalise the lumpen, pickled, salted food of yesteryear. As a result, it's an exciting time to dine out in Reykjavík. Prices are high, but it's worth treating yourself to at least one top-class New Nordic feast while you're here.

The shake-up has trickled down to mid-range restaurants too, which have raised their game in the last decade. In Reykjavík, many restaurants offer good-value fixed-price tourist menus or buffets in summer, with prices lower at lunch (often restricted to around noon–2.30pm). Restaurants in the city tend to be open all day from about 11.30am until 11pm, so you don't have to be too organised about when you eat.

Reykjavík is such a small place, and its streets such a happy jumble, that you can find good places to eat up and down Austurstræti, Hafnarstræti, Laugavegur and the streets that crisscross it. A cluster of excellent seafood restaurants has popped up in the warehouses on Geirsgata. Grandagarður, a little to the north, is an up-and-coming area where you might find interesting new bistros.

Good-quality dining is thinner on the ground outside the capital, and in smaller places, cafés and restaurants may have limited hours (e.g. noon–2.30pm and 7pm–9pm) – it's a good idea to check opening times in advance.

Traditionally, drinking alcohol midweek has not been part of Icelandic culture, although it is becoming more common to have a glass of wine or beer when dining out.

Reykjavík

Austur-Indíafélagið

Hverfisgata 56; tel: 552 1630; www.austurindia.is; daily from 6pm; $$$
Indian spices and Icelandic ingredients turn out to be a perfect match: celebrate the happy marriage at this great little restaurant. Austur-Indíafélagið has some knockout one-of-a-kind dishes, such as tandooried Icelandic langoustines.

Café Paris

Austurstræti 14; tel: 551 1020; www.cafeparis.is; daily from 8.30am; $$
Café Paris sits at the very heart of Reykjavík 101, overlooking Austurvöllur

We have used the following symbols to give an idea of the price for a three-course meal for one, excluding wine:
$$$$ = over ISK10,000
$$$ = ISK5,000–10,000
$$ = ISK2,500–5,000
$ = below ISK2,500

Kaffivagninn, overlooking Reykjavík harbour

square and the Icelandic parliament. People-watchers can enjoy a light lunch, a good cup of coffee and a stream of passersby from the plentiful outdoor tables.

Dill

Hverfisgata 12; tel: 552 1522; http://dill restaurant.is; Wed–Sat from 6pm; $$$

A gourmet's delight, this elegant Scandinavian restaurant specialises in local organic ingredients, cooked in contemporary 'Nordic Kitchen' style. Its five- or seven-course seasonal tasting menus contain dishes such as smoked haddock with blue mussels and reindeer with blueberry sauce.

Fiskfélagið (Fish Company)

Vesturgata 2a, Grófartorg; tel: 552 5300; www.fiskfelagid.is; daily from 5.30pm, plus lunch weekdays; $$$

This atmospheric fusion restaurant gives traditional Icelandic ingredients an international makeover. If you have the stomach space, the seasonal 'Around Iceland' menu provides four courses of the freshest local food, prepared with great skill and imagination.

Gallery Restaurant

Hotel Holt, Bergstaðastræti 37; tel: 552 5700; www.holt.is; closed Sun–Mon; $$$$

Gallery is one of the capital's finest, serving top-notch French-style cuisine: its cured salmon with honey-mustard sauce has been wowing diners for almost 50 years. The largest privately owned art collection in Iceland provides a feast for the eyes.

Gló

Laugavegur 20b; tel: 553 1111; www.glo.is; daily 11am–9pm; $$

Canteen-style Gló, on the second floor, offers fresh, tasty daily dishes (one raw-food; one vegan; one meat), which make use of as many organic ingredients as possible. And if all the virtue gets too much, there's a tempting cake board…

Hornið

Hafnarstræti 15; tel: 551 3340; www.hornid. is; daily 11am–11.30pm; $$

This was the first Italian restaurant to open in Iceland (in 1979), and it has been popular ever since. The atmosphere is relaxed and the pizzas, pasta and fish dishes are good. It gets packed in the evening; reservations are recommended.

Icelandic Street Food

Lækjargata 8; daily 11.30am–9pm; $

Currently one of the most popular spots in town, Icelandic Street Food is fun, friendly, and cheap, and fulfils its small menu to perfection. Delicious soups are served in a filling bread bowl. You'll have to fight for the few tiny tables.

Kaffivagninn

Grandagarði 10; tel: 551 5932; http://kaffivagninn.is; daily until 9pm; $$

Reykjavík's oldest restaurant is located near the harbour, and boasts fantastic views. The menu is short, but there is an excellent choice of Icelandic fish dishes. It's also a good place for breakfast (from 7am Mon–Fri) or Sunday brunch.

Soaking up the sun at Café Paris

Kaffi Vínyl

Hverfisgata 76; tel: 537 1332; www.face
book.com/vinilrvk; daily 8am–11pm; $$
Iceland's first vegan café is laid back
and lots of fun. As well as tasty, whole-
some vegetarian and vegan food – like
baked chickpeas, cinnamon pumpkin,
roast aubergine and tofu – the live DJs
and crackling vinyl collection lends a
funky vibe.

Kol Restaurant

Skólavörðustígur 40; tel: 517 7474;
http://kolrestaurant.is; daily for dinner, Mon–
Fri lunch; $$$$
This small, cosy venue offers an artis-
tic fine-dining experience. See what the
fuss is about with a pretty-as-a-picture
two-course lunch (ISK3,200), or splurge
on the seasonal tasting menu (served
to the whole table only).

Kryddlegin Hjörtu

Hverfisgata 33; tel: 588 8818;
www.kryddleginhjortu.is; daily for dinner,
Mon–Sat lunch; $
The 'Spicy Hearts' restaurant dishes up
bowls of nourishing soup, served with
organic spelt- and barley-bread and a
great salad bar. Main courses flirt with
Indian/Mexican/Middle Eastern fla-
vours. Decent choice for vegetarians.

Lækjarbrekka

Bankastræti 2; tel: 551 4430; www.laekjar
brekka.is; daily from 11.30am; $$$$
In an atmospheric timber building dat-
ing from 1834, Lækjarbrekka is deco-
rated with period furniture, chandeliers
and heavy drapes, and is a classic
choice for a special occasion. Gourmet
set menus feature lobster, lamb and
catch-of-the-day.

Matur og Drykkur

Grandagarður 2; tel: 571 8877; http://matur
ogdrykkur.is; closed Sun lunch; $$$$
In an old salt-fish factory by the harbour,
Matur og Drykkur is absolutely worth
seeking out. Its menu delves deep into
Icelandic culinary history, using modern
methods to raise seaweed, cod's head
and kleina to undreamed of heights.
Reservations strongly recommended.

Ostabúðin

Skólavörðustígur 8; tel: 562 2772;
http://ostabudin.is; daily noon–10pm; $$$
This gourmet delicatessen has a fan-
tastic restaurant attached. A short,
shrewd and well-executed menu tanta-
lises the taste buds – the seafood soup
and catch-of-the-day are some of the
city's best. Table reservations are only
taken up to 7.30pm, so be prepared to
queue.

Snaps

Þórsgata 1; tel: 511 6677; www.snaps.is;
daily from 11.30am; $$$
This bustling bistro-bar is perfect if you
like a bit of a buzz with your steak béar-
naise! Clattering forks and merry chat-
ter bounce around the conservatory-like
interior, warm and inviting. Reserva-
tions are a must.

Corrugated-iron Halldórskaffi

Reykjanes

Lava Restaurant
Blue Lagoon, Grindavík; tel: 420 8800; www.bluelagoon.com; daily 11.30am–9pm; $$$$
Eat overlooking the thermal spa at this world-famous spot. The top-class restaurant cooks up contemporary dishes using local ingredients, such as blue mussels from Reykjanes, Arctic char flavoured with juniper, or creamy skyr with sorrel and rhubarb.

The Southwest

Halldórskaffi
Víkurbraut, Vík; www.halldorskaffi.com; daily noon–9pm or 10pm; $$
Occupying a former 19th-century shop, near the beach, this cheerful café-restaurant gets frenetic in summer. Sunny staff surf the waves of orders, serving hearty portions of pizza, pasta and pan-fried char in a laidback atmosphere.

Rauða húsið
Búðarstígur 4, Eyrarbakki; tel: 483 3330; http://raudahusid.is; dinner daily, plus lunch Fri–Sun; $$$
This is one of the best restaurants on the south coast, with succulent meals and smiling service. The grilled seafood is impressive, and the kitchen vies with rival restaurant Við Fjöruborðið to produce Iceland's best langoustine.

Heimaey

Fiskibarinn
Skólavegur 1; tel: 414 3999; www.facebook.com/fiskibarinn; closed Sun in winter; $$
A fish-and-chip shop with a difference. The short menu features catch of the day, saltfiskur, salmon, Arctic char, smoked haddock and cod tongues, laid out in an ice cabinet so you can see what appeals, then served with brown rice or potatoes.

Gott
Barustígur 11; tel: 481 3060; www.gott.is; Mon–Fri 11am–9pm, Sat–Sun until 10pm; $$$
The former head chef at Iceland's Hilton hotel now runs this fresh, modern restaurant, all in white with pops of bright colour. As well as fish of the day, there are juicy burgers, pulled pork, pastas and steak. Vegan and gluten-free dishes too.

The Southeast

Humarhöfnin
Hafnarbraut 4, Höfn; tel: 478 1200; www.humarhofnin.is; daily from noon; $$$$
Höfn is famous for its lobster (actually langoustines), which is the speciality of this pricey but delicious restaurant in the town's old co-operative building. Portions are generous, and the langoustines come fresh each day from the boats outside.

Kaffi Hornið
Hafnarbraut 42, Höfn; tel: 478 2600; www.kaffihorn.is; daily from 11.30am; $$
The cosiest choice in Höfn, this log cabin by the main road serves large, flavoursome portions of pasta, pizza, burgers and fresh fish at decent prices. It gets very busy in summer.

Fine dining at Hótel Buðir Restaurant

The East Fjords

Café Nielsen

Tjarnarbraut 1, Egilsstaðir; tel: 471 2626; summer only; $$$

This snug café and restaurant in the oldest house in town serves a great choice of dishes. The priciest dish on the menu is regional speciality reindeer, served with blueberries and wild game sauce. There's also a good-value weekday lunch buffet.

The Northeast

Hótel Norðurljós

Aðalbraut 2, Raufarhöfn; tel: 465 1233; www.hotelnordurljos.is; daily 11am–1.30pm and 6–8.30pm; $$

Overlooking the pretty harbour and its fishing boats, this hotel restaurant with outdoor terrace has a superb location. The food here is some of the best in the Northeast – fresh and tasty and making full use of local ingredients.

Kaupvangskaffi

Hafnarbyggð 4a, Vopnafjörður; tel: 662 3588; daily 10am–10pm; $$

There are no other dining options in town; luckily this lovely coffee shop on the main drag serves up excellent grub, from soup of the day to grilled King prawns to its popular Friday lunchtime pizza buffet.

Restaurant Salka

Garðarsbraut 6, Húsavík; tel: 464 2551; salkarestaurant.is; Mon–Fri 11.30am–9pm, Sat–Sun 5pm–9pm; $$

Next to the whale museum, this long-standing restaurant serves fish dishes, pizzas and burgers in a pleasing ambience. There's an outdoor terrace if the weather's good, with harbour views.

Mývatn

Gamli Bærinn

Beside Hotel Reynihlíð, Mývatn; tel: 464 4170; daily 10am–11pm; $$

The name means 'old farm', and the building, which dates from 1912, is by the architect who designed Reykjavík's parliament building. It is a delightful little restaurant and café, where fantastic char soup is served. There's live jazz and local bands at the weekend.

Akureyri & Around

Bautinn

Hafnarstræti 92, Akureyri; tel: 462 1818; www.bautinn.is; daily 9am–11pm; $$

A good choice in the centre of Akureyri for burgers, pizzas, no-nonsense fry-ups and simple meat and fish dishes, with loads of seating, including in the glass conservatory, where you can watch the world pass by.

Rub 23

Kaupvangsstræti 6, Akureyri; tel: 462 2223; www.rub23.is/en; daily dinner, plus Mon–Fri lunch 11.30am–2pm; $$$

This polished fish restaurant is for those who like to play with their food. Choose your trout, lamb, chicken or beef; pick one of 11 marinades; then wait for the chef to cook your special combination.

Fish being smoked   *Colourful Bautinn*

Siglunes

Lækjargata 10, Siglufjörður; tel: 467 1222;
Tue–Sun from 6pm; $$$

For a complete change from the usual small-town fare, try a lamb, chicken or fish tajine at this fabulous place, attached to the guesthouse of the same name. Masterchef Jaouad Hbib uses Icelandic ingredients to rustle up authentic Moroccan dishes.

Strikið

Skipagata 14, Akureyri; tel: 462 7100;
www.strikid.is; Mon–Sat 11am–10pm, Sun 5–10pm; $$$

It might look like an unpromising office block, but this is a good-quality restaurant in the heart of Akureyri with unsurpassed views of the fjord and mountains from its fifth-floor location. Burgers, pizzas, meat and fish dishes.

Veitingastofan Sólvík

Kvosinni, 565 Hofsós; tel: 861 3463;
www.facebook.com/solvikhofsos; 15 May–15 Oct daily 10am–10pm; $$

In a picturesque blue house by the harbour, lovely Sólvík has a varied menu of homecooked food, from huge pancakes to lamb chops and some of the best fish and chips you'll eat.

The Northwest

Ömmukaffi

Húnabraut 2, Blönduós; tel: 452 4040; daily 10am–6pm; $

'Grandma's Café', a buttercup-coloured beacon, makes for a cheerful coffee stop on the long east–west drive through this rather flat, featureless farmland. There are good cakes, or light refreshments like paninis, burgers and an all-you-can-eat soup.

The West Fjords

Hótel Flókalundur

Vatnsfjörður, 451 Patreksfjörður; tel: 456 2011, www.flokalundur.is/dining; mid-May–mid-Sept daily 7.30am–11.30pm; $$$

This is the only restaurant in the vicinity. Rosemary-roasted trout with butter-fried vegetables, roast lamb and garlic lobster are some of the evening meals served. Also a popular coffee stop for people waiting for the ferry to Snæfellsnes.

Við Pollinn

Hótel Ísafjörður, Silfurtorgi 2, Ísafjörður; tel: 456 3360; www.vidpollinn.is; summer daily 11am–9pm, winter Mon–Wed 11am–2pm, Thu–Sat until 9pm; $$$$

The most up-market place to eat in town, with excellent fish dishes and superb views of the fjord. Try the juicy lamb, which melts off the bone.

Snæfellsnes and the West

Hótel Buðir Restaurant

Búðir, 356 Snæfellsbær; tel: 435 6700;
www.hotelbudir.is; summer 6–10pm, winter 6–9.30pm; $$$$

Reopened after a devastating fire, this is one of Iceland's finest hotels. Seafood and game predominate in its oceanfront restaurant, including honey-glazed catfish with ginger, chilli and liquorice sauce.

The stark Art Deco National Theatre

NIGHTLIFE

While there's little of note beyond the capital, Reykjavík is renowned for its lively weekend nightlife, when crowds cram the city's tiny, offbeat bars and pubs for drink, dancing and spontaneous musical happenings. Bar prices are high, so people usually start the party at home – serious clubbing takes place after midnight.

Icelanders smarten up to go out, and long queues form outside the most fashionable places. For up-to-date listings and tips on the 'insider' places to be, check out the irreverent free newspaper *The Reykjavík Grapevine* (www.grapevine.is).

Reykjavík has a thriving cultural scene – *What's On in Reykjavík*, a free monthly listing magazine, includes the latest music, dance and theatre performances. See www.icelandmusic.is for everything you need to know about pop, rock and classical music events across Iceland.

Bars and live music

Austur

Austurstræti 7; www.austurbar.is

Austur is more of a straight-up nightclub than Reykjavík's usual multipurpose café-restaurant-bar-club norm. An upscale crowd gathers to dance to DJs on one of the city's biggest (though still small and crowded!) dance floors. Open Wednesday to Sunday – dress up smart.

Dillon

Laugavegur 30; tel: 821 1111; www.dillon.is

This relaxed rock bar has free entertainment most nights, whether that's a big-screen international football match, regular gigs or legendary sexagenarian DJ Andrea Jónsdóttir, who spins the discs until 3am on Fridays and Saturdays. Dillon has 170+ whiskeys on offer and a nice summer beer garden.

Gaukurinn

Tryggvagata 22; http://gaukurinn.is

One of the biggest venues in downtown Reykjavík, this bar opens every day from 3pm until late. There's a wide range of entertainment on offer, including regular live bands (Icelandic and foreign), burlesque shows and cocktail parties, and weekly English-language stand-up comedy (Monday) and karaoke (Tuesday).

Húrra

Tryggvagata 22; http://hurra.is

In the same building as Gaukurinn, Húrra also has a packed schedule of gigs – from rap to psychedelia – as well as sometime karaoke, short films, themed nights, dance parties, 'drink and draw' events and stand-up comedy. Good beer and a great atmosphere.

Slippbarinn

Mýrargata 2; tel: 560 8080; www.slippbarinn.is

Harpa sparkles at night   *Live music at Dillon*

This slick bar-restaurant, inside the Icelandair Hótel Reykjavík Marína, is a must for jazz fans on Wednesday nights. The local Don Lockwood trio break out guitar, trumpet and double bass and entertain the crowds with a repertoire of jazz standards and the odd original.

Cinema

Bíó Paradís
Hverfisgata 54; tel: 412 7711; www.bioparadis.is
This four-screen central cinema is the antithesis of the bland, impersonal multiplex. Bíó Paradís shows new international and Icelandic independent films, as well as dusting off the classics for your delectation. It's a venue for the Reykjavík International Film Festival, as well as several smaller, specialist film festivals and film-related events.

Concert venues

Harpa Concert Hall
Austurbakki 2; box office tel: 528 5050; www.harpa.is
The city's dazzling harbourside concert hall is home to the Reykjavík Big Band, the Icelandic Opera and the internationally acclaimed Iceland Symphony Orchestra (https://en.sinfonia.is), who perform here from September to mid-June. Designed by Danish-Icelandic artist Ólafur Elíasson, Harpa has become a Reykjavík landmark since its opening in 2011.

Theatre

Iðnó Theatre
Vonarstræti 3; tel: 562 9700; www.idno.is
The first performance at this venerable wooden theatre-by-the-lake took place in 1897. Today it holds six (Icelandic) theatre performances a year, plus a variety of art exhibitions and concerts, from chamber music to burlesque. It often acts as a festival venue, including for Iceland Airwaves.

Mengi
Óðinsgata 2; tel: 588 3644; www.mengi.net
This little venue revels in the experimental, whether that takes the form of music, visual art, dance, theatre or spoken-word performances. Events generally take place on Thursdays, Fridays and Saturdays – see the website for further details. It also has its own record label, releasing innovative examples of rock, electronica, baroque, folk and jazz.

National Theatre
Hverfisgata 19; box office tel: 551 1200; www.leikhusid.is
Iceland's National Theatre was designed, in a peculiarly Icelandic Art Deco style, by state architect Guðjón Samúelsson to resemble a 'Palace of Elves'. It stages 20 to 30 plays, musicals, dance pieces, puppet performances and children's productions every season, around 10 of which are newly commissioned original Icelandic works. The season runs from September to May.

Jökulsárlón glacial lagoon is one of Iceland's most popular attractions

A–Z

A

Age restrictions

The age of consent is 15. You must be at least 18 years old to purchase cigarettes, and at least 20 years old to purchase beer, wine or spirits. The minimum car-rental age is 21 for most car groups (23+ for minivans and 4WDs), and drivers must have held their driving licence for at least one year.

B

Budgeting

Iceland's small population and high import costs make goods and services expensive.

A half-litre of beer at a bar or a glass of house wine at a restaurant costs around ISK1,200. A main course for an evening meal in a budget restaurant costs from ISK3,000; at a moderate restaurant from ISK4,000; at an expensive restaurant from ISK5,000.

In high season, a double room at a basic guesthouse with shared bathrooms costs from ISK12,000; at a moderate hotel around ISK25,000; and at a deluxe hotel around ISK50,000.

The Flybus from Keflavík Airport to Reykjavík city centre costs ISK2,500 (ISK3,000 with hotel drop-off) per person, while the same journey by taxi is around ISK15,000 for one to four people. A single ticket for Reykjavík's city buses costs ISK440, and a one-day travelcard ISK1,560.

The Reykjavík City Card (24/48/72 hours ISK3,700/4,900/5,900) offers free entry to museums, galleries and swimming pools, free bus travel within the capital area, a free ferry trip to Viðey island and discounts for some tours, shops and services.

C

Children

Iceland is a safe, clean, child-friendly country. Most cafés and restaurants provide high chairs. Children are usually charged reduced-price admission fees. In Reykjavík, museum admission is free for under 18s. Very few hotels in Iceland provide baby-sitting services.

Clothing

Iceland's unpredictable weather means that layering is essential. Take a wind- and rainproof coat and a warm sweater, even in summer. Dress well if you plan to visit the city's better restaurants or smarter bars. A swimsuit is crucial so you can enjoy Iceland's many wonderful geothermal bathing pools.

Schoolchildren enjoying the Reykjavík 871±2 Settlement Exhibition

Crime and safety

Iceland is an extremely peaceful and law-abiding nation. Violent crime is virtually non-existent. Petty theft does occur in swimming-pool changing rooms, bars and nightclubs – use common sense, and keep an eye on your bag or wallet.

The biggest threat to visitors is underestimating the terrain and the weather, which can be severe and change rapidly. In recent years, the Icelandic Association for Search and Rescue (ICE-SAR), run entirely by volunteers, has been stretched by tourists behaving recklessly. Hike with proper clothing and equipment, and let someone know where you are going; stick to paths at waterfalls and high-temperature geothermal fields; don't stick your hands in boiling springs; only climb glaciers with proper guidance; and only attempt F-roads in a 4WD vehicle and with proper advice about fording rivers. See safetravel.is for further information.

Customs

Visitors aged 20 and over are allowed to bring in six 'units' of alcohol, where one unit equals: each 0.25 litres of spirits; each 0.75 litres of wine; each three litres of beer. So, for example, you could bring in one litre of spirits (four units) and six litres of beer (two units). As alcohol is expensive, it is worth bringing your full allowance.

Visitors aged 18 and over may bring in 200 cigarettes or 250 grams of tobacco.

On entering or leaving the country, if you are carrying more than €10,000-worth of cash, you must declare it to a customs official.

Visitors to Iceland can claim tax back on purchases of over ISK6,000 – see Money for details.

See www.tollur.is for more information on customs regulations and tax-free shopping.

D

Disabled travellers

Lifts are a rarity, except in major purpose-built hotels. High kerbs, narrow doorways and small rooms can make wheelchair access difficult in Reykjavík's older buildings. Rough terrain and a lack of developed facilities mean wheelchair access to Iceland's natural wonders is rare, although the situation is improving. There are paved paths at Geysir, Gullfoss and Þingvellir National Park, and one leading to the glacier at Skógar.

The public bus system is adapted for wheelchair users. Hertz car hire (tel: 522 4400) and Europcar Holdur (tel: 568 6915) both have larger vehicles with a removable seat where a wheelchair can fit.

All Iceland Tours (tel: 781 2022, www.allicelandtours.is) arrange sightseeing, horse-riding and whale-watching trips for disabled visitors, and the travel agency Iceland Unlimited (tel: 415 0600, icelandunlimited.is) also has specially designed tours.

Björk performing at Iceland Airwaves

Sjálfsbjörg, the Icelandic federation of physically disabled people, can help with queries: tel: 550 0360, email: sjalfsbjorg@sjalfsbjorg.is, www.sjalfsbjorg.is.

E

Electricity

The electric current in Iceland is 220 volts, 50 Hz AC. Plugs are European round pin with two prongs.

Embassies and consulates

Australia: Australian Embassy in Copenhagen, Denmark, tel: (+45) 70 26 36 76, www.denmark.embassy.gov.au.
Canada: Túngata 14, 101 Reykjavík, tel: 575 6500, www.canada.is.
Ireland: Honorary Consul in Reykjavík, Mr David Thorsteinsson, tel: 554 2355, e-mail: davidcsh@islandia.is.
United Kingdom: Laufásvegur 31, 101 Reykjavík, tel: 550 5100, www.gov.uk/world/organisations/british-embassy-reykjavik.
United States: Laufásvegur 21, 101 Reykjavík, tel: 595 2200, https://is.usembassy.gov/embassy/reykjavik.
The Icelandic Foreign Ministry has a full list of diplomatic representatives on its website: www.mfa.is.

Emergencies

For an ambulance, fire service, police or any other emergency, tel: **112** (free from all phones).

Etiquette

If you are invited to an Icelander's home, a small gift is appropriate. It is customary to shake hands when greeting and leaving, and Icelanders always remove shoes before entering anyone's house.

Swimming and bathing places are not usually treated with chemicals, so for hygienic reasons it is vital to wash thoroughly with soap before putting on your swimsuit and entering the water. Failing to do this will cause great offence.

F

Festivals

Some dates change from year to year. Check with tourist offices.
6 January Twelfth Night, marked with songs, bonfires and fireworks.
February Þorrablót. The half-way point of winter, this festival involves eating delicacies including lambs' heads and testicles, and cured shark.
Early February Festival of Lights. Reykjavík's winter festival with arts and cultural events; winterlightsfestival.is.
1st Thursday after 18 April First Day of Summer (*Sumardagurinn fyrsti*). Marked by parades, sports events and the giving of summer-themed gifts.
1st Sunday in June Festival of the Sea (*Sjómannadagur*). Celebrations in all coastal communities with sports and dances.
17 June National Day. Formal ceremonies in the morning and partying and fairs all afternoon and evening, com-

memorating the birth of Iceland as a republic in 1944.

May/June Reykjavík Arts Festival (www. listahatid.is). A two-week celebration of music, theatre, art and dance. Biennial – next in 2018.

Early July Landsmót National Horse Show (www.landsmot.is), held in different towns. Biennial – next in 2018.

1st Monday in August Summer Bank Holiday. A long weekend for all Icelanders, with open-air pop festivals around the country.

August Reykjavík Jazz Festival (http:// reykjavikjazz.is). An annual jazz feast with international stars.

Reykjavík Pride (www.facebook.com/ reykjavikpride). Annual six-day LGBTQ celebration.

September/October Reykjavík Film Festival (www.riff.is). An 11-day extravaganza featuring both Icelandic and international movies.

October/November Iceland Airwaves (www.icelandairwaves.is). A five-day tidal-wave of international indie/pop/rock.

31 December New Year's Eve. A satirical revue on television, followed by night-long outdoor parties with bonfires and fireworks.

H

Health (See also Emergencies)

Thanks to its clean air and low pollution, Iceland is an extremely healthy place. No vaccinations are required to visit Iceland, and the standard of medical care is very high. Iceland's tap water is some of the purest in the world. Avoid bottled water, which is expensive and causes unnecessary plastic waste.

If you are planning to take part in any unusual or 'dangerous' sports, make sure that these are covered by your travel-insurance policy.

Health insurance

An agreement exists between Iceland and countries within the EEA, including the UK, for limited health-insurance coverage of its residents. UK travellers should obtain the European Health Insurance Card (EHIC; www.ehic.org.uk) before leaving home. Remember, the EHIC isn't a substitute for travel insurance.

Pharmacies, hospitals and dentists

There is at least one pharmacy *(apótek)* in every town. Lyfja (Lágmúli 5, Reykjavík, tel: 533 2300) is open daily from 8am–midnight.

For non-emergency medical treatment outside normal hours, the Læknavaktin Medical Centre helpline (tel: 1770) is open Mon–Fri 5pm–8am and 24 hours at weekends. They can provide telephone advice or send a doctor.

The 24-hour casualty department is at Landspítali University Hospital (Fossvogur, tel: 543 2000), or phone an ambulance directly on the emergency number 112.

For an emergency dentist, tel: 575 0505.

Icelandic post is efficient and reliable

Hours and holidays

Opening hours

Opening times are for Reykjavík; elsewhere in the country they may be shorter.

Banks: Mon–Fri 9.15am–4pm.

Offices: Mon–Fri 9am–5pm (June–Aug 8am–4pm).

Post Offices: Mon–Fri 9am–6pm.

Shops: Mon–Fri 9am–5pm/6pm, Sat 10am–1pm/2pm/3pm/4pm. Some supermarkets open until 11pm daily.

Off licenses: Reykjavík: Mon–Thu 11am–6pm, Fri 11am–7pm, Sat 11am–6pm. Other stores usually much shorter hours – see www.vinbudin.is for details.

Public holidays

Most businesses, banks and shops close on public holidays, and public transport is limited.

Fixed dates: 1 January New Year's Day; **1 May** Labour Day; **17 June** National Day; **24 December** Christmas Eve (from noon); **25 December** Christmas Day; **26 December** Boxing Day; **31 December** New Year's Eve (from noon).

Movable dates: March/April Maundy Thursday, Good Friday, Easter Sunday, Easter Monday, First day of summer (first Thursday after 18 April); **May** Ascension Day; **May/June** Whit Sunday, Whit Monday; **August** Bank Holiday Monday (first Monday in August).

Internet facilities

Wi-fi is widely available (free) in cafés, bars and N1 petrol stations. Hotels, guesthouses, libraries and tourist-information offices usually offer internet connection, free or for a small charge.

Language

Nearly all Icelanders speak excellent English.

LGBTQ travellers

Iceland's LGBTQ community has gained legal and social rights that are among the most progressive in the world. The country elected the world's first openly gay prime minister, and passed a gender-neutral marriage bill in 2010.

For information and advice contact: The Gay and Lesbian Association/Samtökin '78, 4th Floor, Suðurgata 3, 101 Reykjavík, tel: 552 7878, e-mail: office@samtokin78.is, www.samtokin78.is. Thursday evenings are 'open night', 8–11pm.

More information about the gay scene can be found at www.gayice.is.

Media

Print

English newspapers and magazines are available in Reykjavík one or two days

Reykjavík Pride, a celebration of the LGBTQ community, lasts for six days

after publication, in bookshops and public libraries.

The magazine *Iceland Review* (www.icelandreview.com) is published in English six times per year, with articles and great photographs. The *Reykjavík Grapevine* (http://grapevine.is), an irreverent, free English-language newspaper containing articles, reviews and listings, is published 21 times per year and is widely available.

Television

The state-run RÚV channels and the pay channel Stöð 2 are the most widely watched home-grown TV channels in Iceland. Some hotels offer satellite TV with international news and entertainment channels including CNN and BBC Worldwide.

Money

Currency: The Icelandic currency is the króna (ISK; plural: krónur). Notes are in denominations of ISK10,000, 5,000, 2,000, 1,000 and 500, coins in ISK100, 50, 10, 5 and 1.

US dollars, sterling and euros are all easily exchanged at banks. Outside normal banking hours, you can exchange money at major hotels. There are 24-hour exchange facilities at Keflavík Airport: look for Landsbankinn in the arrival hall for arriving passengers; on the second level for departing passengers.

At the time of going to press, the rate of exchange was as follows: £1 = ISK144; E1 = ISK127; $1 = ISK108.

Credit and debit cards: Credit and debit cards are used everywhere in Iceland, even for small purchases. US visitors should note that Iceland uses the chip-and-PIN system: double check before travelling that your card will work.

Cash machines: The simplest way to get money is from an ATM cash machine, plentiful in towns. Charges will depend on your bank.

Tipping: Tipping is unnecessary.

Taxes: Visitors can claim tax back as long as they have spent a minimum of ISK6,000 in one transaction and will be taking their purchases home unused. Ask the shop to sign a tax-free form, then take the unused purchases, the completed tax-free form and the original purchase receipts to an international refund point.

P

Post offices

The Icelandic postal service is efficient, and there are post offices (Mon–Fri 9am–6pm) in every town. The Central Post Office on Posthússtræti 5 in Reykjavík is open Mon–Fri 9am–6pm, June, July and August also Sat 10am–2pm. There are up-to-date prices and information at www.postur.is.

R

Religion

Seventy percent of Icelanders belong to the Evangelical Lutheran Church, Iceland's State Church.

S

Smoking

Iceland has the second lowest smoking rate in Europe. Smoking is banned in all public buildings (including bars, clubs, cafés and restaurants).

T

Telephones

The code for Iceland is +354, followed by a seven-digit number. There are no area codes. To call abroad from Iceland, dial 00, plus the country code (Australia +61, Canada +1, Ireland +353, UK +44, US +1).

The cheapest way to make local calls is to buy an Icelandic SIM card and use it in your (unlocked) mobile phone. Prepaid SIM cards, from providers Nova, Síminn and Vodafone, can be bought at filling stations, 10/11 stores and some hotels and tourist offices.

US visitors should check before leaving home whether their phones will work on the GSM 900/1800 network.

Time zones

Iceland is on Greenwich Mean Time (GMT) all year round.

Toilets

Public toilets are rare. It's easiest to buy a coffee at a bar or café and use the toilets as a patron.

Outside Reykjavík, a recent spate of tourists doing their business in public places, car parks and cemeteries has disgusted Icelanders. Plan bathroom breaks, and be prepared to pay a small bathroom charge if necessary.

Tourist information

Reykjavík: Inside City Hall (Tjarnargata 1; tel: 411 6040; www.visitreykjavik.is; daily 8am–8pm).

Akureyri: At Hof Menningarhús (Hof Culture House; Strandgata 12; tel: 450 1050; www.visitakureyri.is; June–mid-Sept daily 8am–6.30pm, May & late Sept Mon–Fri 8am–5pm, Sat–Sun 9am–4pm, Oct–Apr Mon–Fri 8am–4pm).

Websites for regional tourist offices are: www.east.is; www.northiceland.is; www.south.is; www.west.is; www.westfjords.is. Tourist information offices in other towns and villages may close in winter.

Information can be obtained worldwide from www.inspiredbyiceland.com.

Tours and guides

A plethora of organised coach tours run from Reykjavík and elsewhere to major sights. Tours are well run, and many allow you to do some exploring by yourself. Reykjavík Excursions (BSI Bus Terminal, 101 Reykjavík, tel: 580 5400, www.re.is) is the biggest providers of bus tours to the west and southwest of the country.

Transport

Arrival by air

The fastest and cheapest way to get to Iceland is by air. **Icelandair** (www.icelandair.co.uk/www.icelandair.com) is the main

At the foot of Skogafoss

airline serving Iceland, operating from both Europe and North America. In the UK, Icelandair serves Belfast, Birmingham, London Gatwick, London Heathrow, Manchester and Glasgow. In North America and Canada, there are direct flights to: Anchorage (summer only), Boston, Chicago, Denver, Edmonton, Halifax (summer only), Minneapolis, Montreal (summer only), New York, Orlando, Philadelphia (summer only), Portland, Seattle, Tampa, Toronto, Vancouver and Washington.

Budget airline **WOW Air** (wowair.co.uk) has year-round departures from London Gatwick, London Stansted, Bristol and Edinburgh. The airline also flies from US and Canadian destinations, including Boston, Chicago, Cincinnati, Cleveland, Dallas, Detroit, Los Angeles, Miami, Montreal, New York, Pittsburgh, San Francisco, St Louis, Toronto and Washington.

EasyJet (www.easyjet.com) has year-round departures from London Gatwick, London Luton, London Stansted, Belfast, Bristol, Edinburgh and Manchester.

Almost every international flight arrives at **Keflavík International Airport** (tel: 425 6000, www.kefairport.is), 50km (31 miles) from Reykjavík. Flybus (www.re.is/flybus) and Airport Express (https://airportexpress.is) transfer coaches meet each flight, and transport passengers to the BSÍ bus terminal, about 1.5km (1 mile) from the centre of Reykjavík. The journey takes about 45 minutes and costs ISK2,500 per person (ISK3,000 with hotel drop-off): buy tickets from the ticket machine or booth next to the airport exit.

Taxis from the airport to central Reykjavík take 30–45 minutes and cost approximately ISK15,000 for one to four people.

In summer, some international charter flights land at **Akureyri Airport**, 3km (1.9 miles) south of town.

Reykjavík's Domestic Airport (tel: 570 3000) is in the south of the city, with regular buses to/from the city centre.

Arrival by boat

Smyril Line (www.smyrilline.com) operates a year-round ferry service to Iceland, sailing on Saturdays from Hirtshals in Denmark to Seyðisfjörður in eastern Iceland, calling in at Tórshavn (Faroe Islands). In high season (mid-June-mid-Aug), there's a second sailing on Wednesdays direct from Hirtshals to Seyðisfjörður.

Local transport

Buses (city). Reykjavík has an excellent bus system, run by Strætó. Its yellow city buses generally run Mon–Fri 6.30am–11.30pm, Sat 7.30am–11.30pm and Sun 9.30am–11.30pm. There is a flat fare of ISK440, to be paid in exact change as you board. If you are changing buses, ask for a *skiftimiði* (exchange ticket), which is valid on all buses for around 90 minutes. You can also buy a one-/three-day pass for ISK1,560/3,650. Route maps are available from terminals, tourist offices and at www.straeto.is.

Buses (long distance). Some (yellow-and-blue) Strætó buses drive to destinations outside the capital – most leave

The open road

from Mjodd terminal, 8km (5 miles) southeast of the city centre. Long-distance coaches operate from BSÍ Coach Terminal (Vatnsmýrarvegur; tel: 562 1011, www.bsi.is). In summer, Reykja**-Excursions offers various long-distance bus passes – see Iceland on your Own (tel: 580 5400, www.re.is/iceland-on-your-own) for prices and schedules.

Domestic flights. Air Iceland (tel: 570 3030, www.airicelandconnect.com), the biggest domestic carrier, runs flights from Reykjavík's domestic airport to Akureyri, Egilsstaðir and Ísafjörður; and from Akureyri to Grímsey, Þórshöfn and Vopnafjörður. Their 'net offers', booked in advance, can be cheaper than buses.

Eagle Air (Flugfélag Ernir, tel: 562 2640, www.eagleair.is) also operates internal flights from Reykjavík to Bíldudalur and Gjögur in the West Fjords, Húsavík, Höfn and the Vestmannaeyjar.

Ferries. The ferry Herjólfur (tel: 481 2800, www.saeferdir.is) runs to the Vestmannaeyjar, from Landeyjahöfn near Hvollsvöllur on the south coast, or sometimes from Þorlákshöfn in certain wind/tide conditions. Sæferðir (Smiðjustígur 3, 340 Stykkisholmur, tel: 433 2254, www.seatours.is) runs the ferry Baldur, which sails to the West Fjords, as well as whale-watching tours and other excursions. *Sæfari* sails from Dalvík to Grímsey via Hrísey (Samskip, Ranarbraut 2b, 620 Dalvík, tel: 458 8970, www.samskip.is/innanlands).

Taxis. Taxis are available in all the major towns and cost about ISK1,600 for 3km (1.9 miles). There are ranks in Reykjavík on Lækjargata and Eiríksgata (alongside Hallgrímskirkja), but most people book one of the four 24-hour cab companies by phone: Airport Taxi (tel: 420 1212, www.airporttaxi.is); Borgarbílastöðin (tel: 552 2440, www.borgarbilastodin.is); BSR (www.taxireykjavik.is, tel: 561 0000); or Hreyfill (www.hreyfill.is, tel: 588 5522).

Trains. There are no trains in Iceland.

Driving

Driving in Iceland can be a real pleasure – roads are not busy and you have the freedom to go at your own pace. Be prepared for journeys to take a lot longer than you might expect from the distances involved: take your time, and never underestimate road conditions.

Road conditions. While most of the Route 1 encircling the country is surfaced, some routes in Iceland are unmade and full of potholes. Roads may be prone to flooding, bridges are often single-lane, and livestock sometimes make mad dashes into the middle of the road.

Sandstorms can be a hazard along the coast. In winter, snowdrifts, ice and black ice are common. Winter tyres are essential, and studded winter tyres are legal from 1 November to 15 April. For information on road conditions, tel: 1778 or check www.vegagerdin.is. Also see www.safetravel.is.

Rules and regulations. Icelanders drive on the right. The speed limit is 30kmh (18mph) or 50kmh (30mph) in urban areas, 80kmh (50mph) on gravel roads in rural areas and 90kmh (55mph) on asphalt roads out of the towns.

Land of snow and ice   *The ferry Herjólfur*

Off-road driving is illegal – it causes immeasurable damage to Iceland's fragile environment, and fines are extremely high. Seat belts are compulsory in the front and back of a car, and headlights must be used day and night. It is against the law to drive a vehicle in Iceland after consuming any alcohol: drink-drivers lose their licences and face heavy fines. The use of mobile phones while driving is also illegal.

The usual international symbols are used on road signs, but also look out for: einbreið brú (single-lane bridge, often marked by flashing orange lights); malbik endar (beginning of an unmade road); blindhæð (blind summit).

Fuel. In Reykjavík there are several 24-hour filling stations. Those that close overnight usually have automatic pumps that take banknotes or credit cards (but check that yours works while the kiosk is still manned!). Around the Ring Road there are filling stations every 50km (30 miles) or so, but if in doubt fill up before you move on.

Car hire. There are international car-hire companies and locally based firms. You must be at least 21 years old to hire a car. Prices are high. Insurance is compulsory and not always included in the quoted price. Many hire companies offer one-way rentals, allowing you to drive from Reykjavík to Akureyri, for example, and then return by air.

It is worthwhile going over your intended route with the rental company to check what roads are allowed for your type of vehicle. Note that normal cars are not insured for the interior or F-roads.

Parking. Reykjavík has plenty of street parking and car parks, some of which are covered and attended. Parking zones are divided into P1, P2, P3 and P4, with P1 being the most central/expensive. Elsewhere in the country you will encounter few problems, and there are large free car parks at most major tourist sites.

V

Visas and passports

Iceland is a signatory to the Schengen Agreement, so, in principle, residents of other Schengen countries (Norway plus all EU countries except Britain and Ireland) can enter the country with national identity cards rather than passports. Flights from the UK go through passport control. Iceland doesn't require visas from citizens of EU states, the US, Canada, Australia or New Zealand; South African citizens do require one. The normal entry stamp in your passport is valid for a stay of up to 90 days, and your passport must be valid for a further three months beyond your proposed departure date. See www.utl.is for further information.

W

Weights and measures

Iceland uses the metric system.

Women travellers

Iceland is one of the safest countries in the world, and women travelling alone should have no issues.

Fresh produce on sale in Reykjavík

LANGUAGE

About Icelandic

Icelandic is one of the Nordic family of languages and most closely resembles Norwegian and Faroese. Remarkably, the Icelandic spoken today has not changed greatly from the language of the early Norse settlers.

Most Icelanders speak English fluently, as well as Danish, Norwegian or Swedish. German and French are also taught at school. If you can pick up a few phrases of Icelandic, it will be appreciated.

Greetings & basics

There is no word for 'please' in Icelandic. *Gerðu svo vel* is used to invite a person into a house or begin eating. It also means 'here you are' when giving something to somebody. Thank your host by saying *Takk fyrir mig*.

Hello/good morning *Góðan dag*
Good evening *Gott kvöld*
Goodnight *Góða nótt*
What is your name? *Hvað heitir þú?*
My name is... *Ég heiti*
How are you? *Hvað segirðu gott?*
Fine, and you? *Allt fínt, en þú?*
Goodbye *Bless*
Yes *Já*
No *Nei*
Thanks (very much) *Takk (fyrir)*
Yes please *Já takk*
May I have... *Má eg fá...*
Today *Í dag*
Tomorrow *Á morgun*

Yesterday *Í gær*
Cheers! *Skál!*
How much does this cost? *Hvað kostar þetta?*
Excuse me *Afsakið*
Sorry *Fyrirgefðu*
I do not understand *Ég skil ekki*

Signs

Toilet *Snyrting*
Gents *Karlar*
Ladies *Konur*
Open *Opið*
Closed *Lokað*
Danger *Hætta*
Forbidden *Bannað*
Entry *Inngangur/Inn*
Exit *Útgangur/Út*
Parking *Bílastæði*
Airport *Flugvöllur*
Chemist *Apótek*
Doctor *Læknir*
Health Centre *Heilsugæslustöð*
Hospital *Sjúkrahús*
Mechanic/garage *Verkstæði*
Police *Lögreglan*
Post office *Póstur*
Swimming pool *Sundlaug*

Days of the week

Monday *Mánudagur*
Tuesday *Þriðjudagur*
Wednesday *Miðvikudagur*
Thursday *Fimmtudagur*
Friday *Föstudagur*

Bilingual sign at Keflavík International Airport

Saturday *Laugardagur*
Sunday *Sunnudagur*
Weekend *Helgi*

Numbers

Zero *Núll*
One *Einn*
Two *Tveir*
Three *Þrír*
Four *Fjórir*
Five *Fimm*
Six *Sex*
Seven *Sjö*
Eight *Átta*
Nine *Níu*
Ten *Tíu*
Twenty *Tuttugu*
One hundred *Hundrað*
One thousand *Þúsund*

Internet

Mobile phone *Farsími*
Tablet *Spjaldtölva*
Laptop *Fartölva*
Internet *Internet*
Wi-fi *Þráðlaus tenging*
Username *Notandi*
Password *Lykilorð*
E-mail *Tölvupóstur*
To log in/out *Að skrá inn/út*
To charge (a phone etc) *Að hlaða*

At the restaurant

I would like... *Ég ætla að fá...*
Have you got any...? *Áttu til...?*
No more, thank you *Ekki meira takk*
I am vegetarian *Ég er grænmetisæta*
The bill, please *Reikninginn, takk*

Menu *Matseðill*
Starters *Forréttir*
Soup *Súpa*
Bread *Brauð*
Butter *Smjör*
Sugar *Sykur*

Kjötréttir/meat dishes
Meat *Kjöt*
Lamb *Lambakjöt*
Beef *Nautakjöt*
Pork *Svínakjöt*
Chicken *Kjúklingur*
Smoked lamb *Hangikjöt*

Fiskréttir/fish dishes
Fish *Fiskur*
Haddock *Ýsa*
Prawns *Rækjur*
Salmon *Lax*
Trout *Silungur/Bleikja*

Grænmeti/vegetables
Potatoes *Kartöflur*
Chips *Franskar*
Peas *Grænar baunir*
Cabbage *Rauðkál Red*
Mushrooms *Sveppir*
Carrots *Gulrætur*
Salad *Salat*

Drykkir/drinks
Tea *Te*
Coffee *Kaffi*
Milk *Mjólk*
Beer *Bjór*
White/red wine *Hvít-/rauðvín*
Water *Vatn*

The Icelandic sagas were only recorded in the 13th and 14th centuries

BOOKS AND FILM

Iceland's proud literary heritage is most famously captured in the medieval sagas, historical chronicles, romances and legends committed to vellum in the 13th and 14th centuries. Best known are the family sagas, 40 or so sprawling stories about the lives and struggles of the early settlers. They offer a fascinating glimpse into a semi-pagan mindset, where oathbreaking, meanness and cowardice are the worst sins, and where fate is the strongest force in determining how the characters live and die. Many of Iceland's sagas have been translated into English and other languages; particularly readable are *Egils Saga*, *Laxdæla Saga* and *Njáls Saga*, all published under the Penguin Classics label.

By far the most important modern literary figure is Halldór Laxness, winner of the 1955 Nobel Prize for Literature. Laxness portrayed the dark underside of rural life: his best-known creation is Bjartur, the stubborn peasant protagonist of *Independent People*.

Iceland has a pretty respectable film industry for a country of only 335,000 people. Friðrik Þór Friðriksson is one of the most influential filmmakers in Europe, and Baltasar Kormákur has directed several international crowd-pleasers.

A host of foreign films and television series make use of Iceland's oth-erworldly landscape, including *Game of Thrones*, *Stars Wars* (*Rogue One* and *The Force Awakens*), *Sense8*, *Interstellar*, *Thor: The Dark World*, *Prometheus*, *Stardust*, *Batman Begins* and James Bond movies *Die Another Day* and *A View to a Kill*.

Books

Non-fiction
Cod: A Biography of the Fish that Changed the World by Mark Kurlansky. Highly acclaimed, fascinating account of a fish so vital to Iceland.
A Guide to the Flowering Plants and Ferns of Iceland by Hörður Kristins-son. A comprehensive full-colour identification guide, written by the former Professor of Botany at the University of Iceland.
Icelandic Bird Guide by Jóhann Óli Hilmarsson. A practical guide to identifying Icelandic breeding birds, visitors, vagrants, eggs and fledglings.
Icelandic Food & Cookery by Nanna Rögnvaldardóttir. Icelandic cookbook, for a literal taste of Iceland.
Last Places: A Journey in the North by Lawrence Millman. An extremely funny travelogue, which exactly pinpoints the attraction of cold, bleak landscapes.
Letters from Iceland by W.H. Auden and Louis MacNeice. Irreverent letters and poems sent by the two poets

Unsettling scene in Jar City

in 1936, still fascinating and funny today.

Ring of Seasons by Terry Lacy. A good all-round overview of Icelandic history and culture from the perspective of a foreign resident.

Fiction

101 Reykjavík by Hallgrimur Helgason. A comic tale of a middle-aged man-child in a bizarre love triangle.

The Blue Fox by Sjón. A short, strange fable by playwright, poet and some-time-Björk-collaborator Sjón.

Burial Rites by Hannah Kent. Based on the true story of Agnes Magnúsdóttir, the last person to be executed in Iceland.

Fish Have No Feet by Jón Kalman Stefánsson. A moving family saga, spanning a century of Icelandic history.

Independent People by Halldór Laxness. Must-read classic satire of a man's struggle for independence, by a Nobel Prize-winning author.

The Sagas of the Icelanders, translated by Robert Kellogg. Includes 10 sagas and seven shorter Old Norse tales.

Icelandic Noir

Nine of **Arnaldur Indriðason's books** featuring Reykjavík detective Erlendur have been translated into English: *Jar City, Silence of the Grave, Voices, The Draining Lake, Arctic Chill, Hypothermia, Outrage, Black Skies* and *Strange Shores*.

Siglufjörður is the setting for **Ragnar Jónasson's 'Dark Iceland' series:** *Snowblind, Nightblind, Blackout* and *Rupture*.

Yrsa Sigurðardóttir sends her protagonist, lawyer Þóra Guðmundsdóttir, to investigate nefarious deeds in *Last Rituals, My Soul to Take, Ashes to Dust, The Day is Dark, Someone To Watch Over Me* and *The Silence of the Sea*.

Films

101 Reykjavík (2000). Directed by Baltasar Kormákur, this award-winning film is based on the darkly comic book of the same name.

Angels of the Universe (2000). Sometimes called the Icelandic *One Flew Over the Cuckoo's Nest*, this film charts a young man's slide into madness.

Children of Nature (1991). Iceland's urbanisation provides the backdrop to a stirring story of old age, friendship and freedom.

The Deep (2012). The incredible true story of fisherman Guðlaugur Friðþórsson's fight for survival, after his boat capsizes off the Westman Islands.

Jar City (2006). Ingvar E. Sigurðsson stars as gloomy Reykjavík detective Erlendur, investigating a murder with a genetic twist.

Rams (2015). Iceland's biggest international box-office hit. In this tragicomedy, two battling brothers, Gummi and Kiddi, maintain a 40-year silent standoff, until a threat to their beloved sheep changes the stakes.

ABOUT THIS BOOK

This *Explore Guide* has been produced by the editors of Insight Guides, whose books have set the standard for visual travel guides since 1970. With top-quality photography and authoritative recommendations, these guidebooks bring you the very best routes and itineraries in the world's most exciting destinations.

BEST ROUTES

The routes in the book provide something to suit all budgets, tastes and trip lengths. As well as covering the destination's many classic attractions, the itineraries track lesser-known sights. The routes embrace a range of interests, so whether you are an art fan, a gourmet, a history buff or have kids to entertain, you will find an option to suit.

We recommend reading the whole of a route before setting out. This should help you to familiarise yourself with it and enable you to plan where to stop for refreshments – options are shown in the 'Food and Drink' box at the end of each tour.

For our pick of the tours by theme, consult Recommended Routes for… (see pages 6–7).

INTRODUCTION

The routes are set in context by this introductory section, giving an overview of the destination to set the scene, plus background information on food and drink, shopping and more, while a succinct history timeline highlights the key events over the centuries.

DIRECTORY

Also supporting the routes is a Directory chapter, with a clearly organised A–Z of practical information, our pick of where to stay while you are there and select restaurant listings; these eateries complement the more low-key cafés and restaurants that feature within the routes and are intended to offer a wider choice for evening dining. Also included here are some nightlife listings, plus a handy language guide and our recommendations for books and films about the destination.

ABOUT THE AUTHOR

Fran Parnell's passion for Iceland and Scandinavia began while studying Norse and Celtic at Cambridge University. She has also written guides to Sweden, Finland and Denmark.

CONTACT THE EDITORS

We hope you find this Explore Guide useful, interesting and a pleasure to read. If you have any questions or feedback on the text, pictures or maps, please do let us know. If you have noticed any errors or outdated facts, or have suggestions for places to include on the routes, we would be delighted to hear from you. Please drop us an email at hello@insightguides.com. Thanks!

CREDITS

Explore Iceland
Editor: Helen Fanthorpe
Author: Fran Parnell
Head of Production: Rebeka Davies
Update Production: Apa Digital
Picture Editor: Aude Vauconsant
Cartography: Carte
Photo credits: Alamy 91L, 110/111T, 115, 116/117, 118/119, 121, 122, 123L, 139; Arctic Adventure/ellithor.com 60/61; David Leffman/Rough Guides 15L; Diana Jarvis/Rough Guides 8MR, 18, 19L, 26/27, 110MR; Getty Images 6MC, 7M, 18/19, 21, 26, 28/29T, 31, 35L, 34/35, 36/37, 45, 88/89, 100/101, 110ML, 110MR, 112, 113, 124, 125L, 128, 131, 135L, 136, 138; iStock 4ML, 4MR, 4MR, 4/5T, 6TL, 6BC, 7T, 7MR, 8ML, 8MC, 8MR, 8/9T, 10/11, 13, 14, 14/15, 17L, 23, 28MR, 28ML, 28MR, 32, 34, 38/39, 40, 50/51, 53, 54, 56, 56/57, 62/63, 64, 65, 73, 74/75T, 76, 77L, 76/77, 78, 80, 87, 90/91, 94, 98/99, 100, 101L, 104B, 104T, 105, 107, 108, 109L, 110ML, 110MC, 122/123, 124/125, 126, 130, 132/133, 134, 134/135, 137; James Macdonald 46; Karl Petersson/Rough Guides 16, 16/17; Melkorka Magnúsdóttir/wphallus.is 4ML; Ming Tang-Evans/Apa Publications 4MC, 7MR, 8ML, 8MC, 22, 28ML, 28MC, 28MC, 30, 33L, 32/33, 42/43, 50, 51L, 52, 66, 67L, 69, 70/71, 72, 79, 81, 82/83, 92, 93, 96, 97; Rough Guides 110MC, 127; Shutterstock 4MC, 6ML, 13, 20, 24/25, 27L, 41, 42, 43L, 44, 47, 48/49, 55, 57L, 58, 59, 66/67, 68, 74B, 84, 85, 86/87, 90, 95L, 94/95, 102/103, 106, 108/109, 114, 129; Stefan Auth/imageBROKER/ REX/Shutterstock 120; Völundur Jónsson/ wiceland.is 1
Cover credits: iStock (main) Shutterstock (bottom)

Printed by CTPS – China

DISTRIBUTION

UK, Ireland and Europe
Apa Publications (UK) Ltd
sales@insightguides.com
United States and Canada
Ingram Publisher Services
ips@ingramcontent.com
Australia and New Zealand
Woodslane
info@woodslane.com.au
Southeast Asia
Apa Publications (Singapore) Pte
singaporeoffice@insightguides.com
Worldwide
Apa Publications (UK) Ltd
sales@insightguides.com

SPECIAL SALES, CONTENT LICENSING AND COPUBLISHING

Insight Guides can be purchased in bulk quantities at discounted prices. We can create special editions, personalised jackets and corporate imprints tailored to your needs. sales@insightguides.com
www.insightguides.biz

INDEX

MAP LEGEND

- ● Start of tour
- — Tour & route direction →
- ❶ Recommended sight
- ❷ Recommended restaurant/café
- ★ Place of interest
- ❶ Tourist information

- ✈ Airport
- – – – Ferry route
- ⚑ Statue/monument
- ✚ Church
- ✉ Main post office
- 🚌 Main bus station
- ✚ Hospital
- ✳ Viewpoint

- ⚑ Lighthouse
- ◠ Volcano
- ⬧ Cave
- Park
- Important building
- Transport hub
- Pedestrian area
- Urban area